CW01677448

Flying made my arms ache

FLYING

MADE MY

ARMS ACHE

BY

R.W. "Wally" Wallens DFC
Squadron Leader RAF (Ret'd)

A few of the rather rambling reminiscences
of a fighter pilot

Published in 1990 by
The Self Publishing Association Ltd
Lloyds Bank Chambers,
Upton-upon-Severn, Worcs.
A MEMBER OF

in conjunction with
WALLY WALLENS
Flat 3, 13 Avenue Road,
Stratford-upon-Avon,
Warks.

© Wally Wallens 1990

This book is copyright. No part of it may be reproduced in any form without prior permission in writing from the publishers except by a reviewer who wishes to quote brief passages in connection with a review written for inclusion in a newspaper, magazine, radio or television broadcast.

British Library Cataloguing in Publication Data
Wallens, Wally
Flying made my arms ache
1. World War 2. Air operations by Great Britain. Royal Air Force. Pilots – Biographies
I. Title
940.544941092

ISBN 1 85421 081 5

Designed and Produced by The Self Publishing Association Ltd
Printed and Bound in Great Britain by Billing & Sons Ltd, Worcester

CONTENTS

To Vicky, my lovely wife,

and

Karen my dear daughter

for everything

Song – Poem

Forty years on, when afar and asunder,
Parted are those who are singing today.
When we look back and regretfully wonder,
What we were like in our work and our play.

Harrow School Song

FOREWORD
by
Keith Fordyce. MA

The Radio and TV personality, one of the founders, and Curator, of the Torbay Aircraft Museum, Higher Blagdon, Nr Paignton, Devon. (now temporarily closed pending proposed re-siting in Torbay).

Skills, problems and pressures – none of these words would readily be associated with a fourth – humour. The reader of this book will soon learn, surely to his delight, that the warm and winning sense of humour of Wally Wallens ranks equally with his description and understanding of the skills required, the problems encountered and the pressures endured by a pilot in the second world war.

What's more, here are three stories in one. Flying before and during the Battle of Britain qualifies Wally as one of the elite – 'The Few'. Later, as CO of No. 1 Aircraft Delivery Flight, he was called upon to demonstrate his excellence as a pilot in the handling of a wide variety of types of aircraft. His posting to duties in Air Sea Rescue, and his love-hate relationship with the Walrus flying-boat, make the third story – equally intriguing and, at times, nail-biting.

I first met Wally, quite by chance, in a pleasant old South Devon pub some 10 years ago. Since then I have greatly treasured the privilege of his friendship, which has been both well-cemented and generously liquified! My affection for him extends to his wife Vicky, and their adventuresome daughter, Karen.

When Winston Churchill uttered his memorable tribute to 'The Few' he may have been recalling another era of great danger to the British Isles – the threat posed by the Spanish Armada some 350 years earlier. In anticipation of this threat, Queen Elizabeth the First gave orders for suitable fortifications to be built on St Mary's in the Isles of Scilly. It was Sir Francis Godolphin who was given the task of organising the construction of Star Castle, which still stands intact to this day. In a report to the Queen on the completion of the work, Sir Francis wrote:

> "So much has seldom been performed at such small charge and with so few hands in so short a time."

Higher Blagdon 1989

PREFACE

The boyhood dream – that of becoming a fighter pilot in the RAF.

When I was so very young I was fascinated by the deeds of the 'Aces' of the air battles of the 1914-18 War – Ball, Bishop, Mannock, McCudden, the Frenchman Fonck, the German, the Red Baron Richtofen, the American Rickenbacker, and many others. I knew them all, their aircraft, their score of victories, and never tired of reading of their exploits.

For me the dream never faded, stirred by a flight in an Avro 504K, warmed by the visit of Alan Cobham's Aerial Circus, and it became an obsessive ambition the day in the early thirties when Flying Officer Hay, our history master, landed his gleaming RAF biplane on the playing fields at my school, Worksop College.

From then on my mind was made up – I declined to go up to University, I scorned a business career. There was but one future for me, the Royal Air Force, the desire to fly fighters. Nothing would deter me, and so, for what it is worth, my story begins.

Many others, better qualified than I, have written about the air war of 1939-45, of the outstanding pilots, and of the strategy and tactics of Fighter Command, particularly during the Battle of Britain, which was, after all, a minor phase in the whole global conflict during those long years, yet having some influence on the eventual outcome.

I do not think that the majority of young fighter pilots engaged in the Battle, particularly in 11 Group, ever considered that this period was to be so critical that total defeat and the tyranny of occupation by the German forces might be a possibility.

The first sight of very large formations of German bombers, with massive fighter escorts, sweeping across the Channel, over the South Coast and up the Thames was an awesome, evil sight that aroused the most intense resentment.

Very few thought too long about the obvious odds that had to be faced. There was an attitude of calmness and resolution, and a simple conviction and determination that the fighter squadrons of the RAF would not be found wanting. In the event, many brave men from all corners of the British Empire died in the bitter struggle, and I am very proud and honoured that I had the good fortune to fly and fight in their company.

They were professionals, led by professionals, confident and dedicated, with an intense pride in the Service, their Squadrons and their aircraft, but would as the opportunity arose and with the exuberance of youth, get up to any mad escapade or prank that their fertile minds could evolve. A letting-off of steam on which authority would frown, rarely admonish, and laugh at the re-telling. It is of some of these boys, which most were, that I write to honour their memory.

I have rarely consulted any diaries, authors' works, reference books, official records or log books, relying almost entirely on my memory to recall some interesting incidents, and many others, equally interesting but, regrettably, quite unprintable.

These have all flooded back with vivid clarity, as if it were yesterday and not years ago, and I can but hope that my stories may raise just the flicker of a smile.

Finally, I would pay the highest tribute possible to the men on the ground, the NCOs and Airmen, fitters, riggers radio-technicians and armourers who toiled day and night, often in the most dangerous conditions, to keep our aircraft flying when airfields were being plastered with German bombs.

They were the true 'Unsung' whose superhuman efforts made it all possible, but who were rarely given the full recognition and awards which they so richly deserved.

The Royal Air Force, from its inception to the present day, has led the Air Forces of the World and none can deny that its motto *Per Ardua ad Astra* is the finest of them all.

Squadron Leader R.W. "Wally" Wallens DFC

SPITFIRE 1940

The Spitfire was dying. Not quickly, in the shattering, explosions of direct hits ripping apart man and machine in a fiery, bloody disintegration. Not even peacefully, engineless and cannibalised; retired to a compound, to stand forlorn and watch its successors roar above. But dreadfully, in a gut-grinding screech of tormented engine metals white-hot and melting, jerking and shuddering in a dance of disaster across the sky, shedding its skin of metal and control fabric, snorting clouds of oily smoke, and dropping inexorably to the waiting ground below.

The pilot sat hunched in the cockpit, dirty, soaked with sweat, and feeling the cold chills of panic, striving to force his mind, the trained mind of experience, to concentrate on the frightening task ahead.

He knew that the long cannon shell burst that ripped into him when the 109 'jumped' him, had wrecked his rudder. His elevator and ailerons felt sloppy but responsive and he had broken away violently to port in instantaneous evasive reaction praying that his aircraft would stay in control.

It had, and he had turned and climbed up-sun as best he could with full throttle, the Merlin engine hammering, vibrating and threatening to tear itself from its bearers. He was forced to throttle back to low boost pressure and revolutions and level off.

The 109 had lost him and he had time to review his

chances of survival. The top surface of his mainplanes were a honeycomb of torn metal and he assumed that his hydraulics were probably gone as his pressure gauge, along with the majority of the instruments before him lay in a shattered, unrecognisable mess. It meant a wheels-up landing.

His leg felt numb but he could see when he tugged his tattered trouser that the cannon shell had blasted his leg but not severed it, the blood welling from the wound and over his shoe onto the rudder pedal and into the fuselage below.

The radio control on his left had disappeared in the burst of fire that ruled out a 'Mayday' call for assistance and he thought grimly, "Who the bloody hell can help me now anyway?"

Experience told him that the Jerry, luckily for him, must be a new boy or getting sloppy. Although accurate he had fired from out of range and the cannon shells had not been effective enough to burst his back and head armour and kill him, although they had jammed his canopy channels. He could not get out, he was stuck with it and there was only one way – and that was down.

He headed in over the Foreland and up the Thames, losing power and height, frightened to open the throttle in case the labouring engine blew up in his face, praying that his P for Peter would get him back to base, now only a few miles ahead.

The signs of break-up came suddenly with white clouds of glycol pouring from the header tank and, as the power faded, he rammed the throttle wide open, looking over the side to judge his altitude and find a field suitable for the emergency landing.

The billowing glycol stream obscured his forward vision completely so he looked over his shoulder sideways to port and starboard, knowing with dread that if he found what he wanted he must make a violent steep turn at low altitude, down wind with a very sick engine and remain at right angles to his chosen landing area to the last moment before straightening up and committing himself to that final approach and touch down, unseeing.

The perspiration, hot yet cold, poured down his face within his oxygen mask and from under his helmet into his eyes and he could feel it seeping down his back from his shoulders.

The engine screamed in agony to a halt and his hand had quickly throttled back, flicked ignition switches down, pushed down the fuel levers to 'OFF' and was seeking the flap select control before he realised he dare not select 'flaps down'. If pressure remained, one only might operate and he would smear himself in a spectacular flick roll into the ground. Also it must be a wheels-up landing and, he knew, flaps would increase the already excessively steep angle of glide and the change of altitude to flatten out low down in the turn could only increase the hazards, although he would be coming in much faster.

His luck held – a field appeared under the trailing edge of his port wing and he was turning quickly to line up as the adjoining field came into view.

Height was now what – roughly 300 feet, speed in the turn 140-150? Too fast for a normal approach turn but the Spitfire was going down like a brick, as if no lift on the mainplanes existed and shaking as if it would stall and spin at any time. "God", he thought, "Am I right, am I about to go in head first, am I good enough to handle this one"?

He disciplined his rising fears and pulled down hard on his harness straps until they dug into his shoulders and held him rigid.

Behind the stuffy sticky oxygen mask he drew a harsh breath, mouth open, and the sweat from his top lip sucked into his mouth and eased his parched tongue.

NOW, NOW, NOW, is the time to straighten up and put the nose down, height 20 feet? speed about 120, the hedge flashing just below and the end of it all very close now.

The Spitfire was going very fast and level as it touched the ground and, as if striving hopelessly to fly again, it bounded into the air. He pushed hard forward on the control column and the aircraft settled back onto the ground and the crunch became a continuous roaring, rending, earth-churning ride on a terrifying roller coaster. Control went and the pilot sat, helpless, mind-numbed with the hell of it all, crouched as if for protection as P for Peter shattered the hedge, leapt a shallow ditch and slithered, without apparent loss of momentum, towards a row of trees.

"My bloody luck, my bloody rotten luck", and he cursed the trees that blocked his path, closed his eyes and waited, interminably it seemed for the last cruel shattering blow.

He sensed the silence of the hot summer afternoon as he opened his eyes again, the foliage of the trees shading him, the trunk of an oak barely five feet from the nose of the Spitfire.

The crackling of hot metals under the cowlings, – the

death rattle of P for Peter, the shouts of rescuers running across the next field to release him.

The Pilot sat back and waited, the tension and fear draining slowly from him, knowing that this time he would be alright, but there would be others, and the fear returned.

* * *

This story was written in the Spring of 1941 in Hill End Hospital, St Albans, where the author was still recovering after being wounded and crash-landing his Spitfire in September 1940.

Wally's Spitfire 'P' for Peter

Chapter 1

EFTS Perth

The mid-1930s, the unbelievably near-deserted roads, and my nearly new resplendent Austin 7 Tourer (which second-hand had cost just over £20, including the tax and insurance) took me, if not swiftly, safely from my home in Worcestershire to Scone Aerodrome, Perth, Scotland, where my pilot training as a very new Acting Pilot Officer in the Royal Air Force was to start.

'Clara'

Arriving on a wet Sunday morning, after a two day trip at an excellent average speed of 25 mph, I drove up the main drive, flanked by small, neat, bungalows, one of which would become my home for the next three months, and stopped the car alongside the small control tower. Standing in the rain I watched nothing take off and nothing land, my head and heart in the scurrying low clouds, with the miracle soon to happen – I was to learn to fly on this very airfield. Through my closed eyes I performed flawless aerobatics in a Tiger Moth, my instructor and fellow pupils mouths agape at my dexterity and finesse, until the rain that had collected in the brim of my Trilby hat ran over the edge and down my neck, bringing me back to earth.

I reported for duty at Scone Aerodrome the following morning. In my suitcase was a small horseshoe given to me by a wise, far-seeing old lady who assured me that it would be my talisman and take me safely (about which at later times I was to be in some considerable doubt!) through my flying career. I still have that old horseshoe today, and I do believe the old dear could see the future more clearly than I.

My flying instructor, Mr Jarrett was an equable, calm, quiet, gentleman who guided me from my first familiarisation flight, through patient dual instruction and correction and who I thought would never coax my hands and feet to co-ordinate, as did his with such apparent lack of concentration and effort.

However, as a good instructor, he persevered and I can still hear his voice through the Gosport tubes to my helmet, cajoling, threatening, pleading and rarely complimenting, my ham-fisted handling of the long-suffering labrador of a Tiger Moth, which I am sure, left to its own devices, could have made a better job of it than I. In front of me I can see his head and broad shoulders, and his hands on the cockpit cowling, his fingers drumming to a silent song while I proceeded daily to bend stretch and almost break every plate, rib, rivet and fabric part in my frenetic thrashing and heaving in the rear cockpit to master the impossible task of flying that gentle aeroplane.

* * *

None of my fellow pupils had, as yet, gone solo and I had visions of being the last, if ever, to do so, when we took off as usual one morning. Mr Jarrett seemed quieter than usual, letting me get on with my work in the 'boiler room' and, after two bone-crunching, teeth-loosening arrivals, I taxied back down-wind, stopped and Mr Jarrett sat hunched in the front seat, fumbling in his lap. Then, without a word, he dropped the cockpit side flap, stepped out onto the lower wing, still wearing his parachute, reached into the cockpit (to secure the harness straps, although I did not realise this) and took another step down onto the grass.

Unclasping his parachute he took a quick pace to my cockpit put his head forward over the rim and clearly above the propeller's tick over, shouted, "It's a nice morning to be alone – Off you go!" I sat there, aghast, as he strolled round the tailplane, his chute across his shoulder and, a few paces away, took out his pipe and slowly started to fill it, looking anywhere, thank God, but in my direction.

An hour or two later, it seemed, I awoke with a shock, feeling such a bloody fool, and realised that the moment, so long awaited with restless eagerness and fearful trepidation, had come. I was alone, at last, and, flushing like a schoolboy, pulled myself together and started the take-off drill. Controls free, cheese-cutter (the elevator trim) to take off position, fuel check on the upper wing gauge, and, remembering in time to look over my shoulders into the sky for aircraft approaching to land, knew that this was where it was all to begin.

Taking a deep breath, which I think I held until after I landed, I opened the throttle with my left hand, slowly and steadily to take off position. My right hand was on the control column, (the stick) which slowly became heavier and positive as the air flow streamed over the tail-plane, and which I moved carefully forwards from fully back to a centre position as the Tiger Moth accelerated and my feet, moving from left to right to keep a straight line, holding the rudder pedals firmly in the centre position as I gathered speed. The tail came up quickly and I held the Tiger on a light firm rein of exquisite pleasure and restrained excitement as it rumbled its wheels on the grass and with a last light bump lifted me smoothly from the ground and climbed into the sky.

The engine was singing happily, revelling with me in the joy of it all. I heard a voice joining the Gypsy engine in its song and realised it was me and smiled sheepishly but the Tiger carried on, only lowering its voice as I throttled back to climbing revolutions as the airfield boundary slid below.

I could now see forward through the arc of the propeller, the view no longer restricted by the helmeted head and leather coated shoulders of Mr Jarrett. A tremor of apprehension went through me as I realised that Mr Jarrett was back down there on the grass, watching me like a hawk, ready to tear me apart if I did not justify his confidence and bring the Tiger down in one whole piece. I immediately postponed consideration of that part of the flight and concentrated on the job in hand, which was to keep the Tiger on an even keel as the horizon widened in my climb. The mountains were far over to my left and the Tay winding down to Dundee below my right shoulder, and a wonderful sense of total freedom and joy of living encompassed me.

It was time to level off, which I accomplished with confident aplomb. I started my turn to the left at rate 1 to 2, the Tiger skittering as my turn and bank indicator informed me and my body pressed alternately, in the slide out and slip in, against the fuselage. I completed my turn and looked over my left shoulder for the aerodrome. To my relief it had not moved, and it now demanded my next turn on to the downwind leg, which I performed more tidily. I throttled back slightly, mentally laid out my prayer mat, joss sticks, rabbits feet, good luck horseshoes and all the other conglomerate fetishes of those of little faith and, looking down at the windsock to judge wind strength on the surface and searching for other aircraft in the approach, turned port again on to the base leg, losing height progressively, keeping my airspeed steady and trimming back slightly on the elevator control.

I think the Tiger and Mr Jarrett, wanted to get it all over quickly now as the controls moved, seemingly of their own accord into the left turn on to final approach and I was lined up nicely, letting the airspeed fall off as I throttled back a little more, picking a touch down point as near to Mr Jarrett as I dared. The near boundary was just ahead so it was time to throttle fully back, trim and glide in over the fence, the Tiger floating gracefully down, the churned grass coming up to meet me as I pulled the stick farther back until it rested in my groin and the aeroplane, reluctant to return to earth remained suspended until the wheels touched, the tail skid rattled as it gouged the grass and the Tiger and I rolled along and slowly came to rest. That deep breath I had taken some hours before it seemed, whooshed from my throat. I smiled to myself, the smirk of smug satisfaction as I looked about me before taxi-ing slowly to the aircraft line in front of the hangar and switching off my magneto switches and fuel. Talk about pride before the fall, I little knew what was to come.

Tiger Moths

* * *

Mr Jarrett was at my shoulder as I climbed from the cockpit. He looked at me, I'm sure with faintly disguised pride in his eyes, as he growled "Not bad, not bad, I've seen worse though not much but I will tell you something. At this moment you are now the most dangerous member of the species. You think you can fly an aeroplane, but you are sadly mistaken. You are a ham-fisted, egotistical, over-confident, unco-ordinated heap of nothing and you will now begin to learn, and learn and learn until I have knocked off all your rough edges and made a pilot of you and then, and only then, can you permit yourself that idiotic grin. Come along, you can treat me to a shandy. We've taken first wicket."

My cup was full beyond overflowing and, as we strolled across the grass, I'm sure the Tiger waved to me in sympathy as it teetered from side to side in the gentle wind.

* * *

The flying programme, though unremitting and demanding was occasionally relieved when the instructor would either give a brief and polished exhibition of aerobatics or fly fairly low to point out places of interest, and allow one to do a bit of low flying, an exhilerating pastime but not to be carried out willy-nilly to cause annoyance.

One day, after several satisfactory runs, Mr Jarrett let me fly the aircraft at low level down the Tay. It was normal drill to give the fishing boats a mild beat-up and I headed towards one boat, settling down as close to the water as I dared. As the Tiger approached the boat, figures on the deck grew larger and to my surprise, one, burly, bearded character, was swinging something round his head like a hammer-thrower in the Highland Games. Too late, I saw that he was heaving what must have been his largest catch ever, the fish whistling round his head like a silver streak. The fisherman was obviously berserk at our annoying intrusion of peace and privacy, and bent on our destruction.

I have never seen a whale but I swear that this was Moby Dick's brother, as, with a last gargantuan, lung-bursting heave, the fisherman let go. This Zeppelin of a fish soared into the air, climbing like a rocket, head first, in front of the Tiger and I swear that it winked at us as it missed the aircraft by a scales breadth and sank back down and into the river. Had it struck us it would have been not unlike a battleship's broadside and bears not thinking about.

I felt Mr Jarrett's hands and feet on the controls and a calm voice come through my earphones. "I like fishing but this is bloody ridiculous, and if it's sardines on toast for tea I'll probably murder the steward. Let's go home." Away we climbed over the Carse of Gowrie and the Sidlaw Hills to Perth, leaving the poor, tortured fisherman to bemoan his aim and his luck.

* * *

The first few exciting weeks of flying training had passed. From an assortment of young men from Great Britain and the Empire I had formed a light-hearted association with several including Al, a Canadian who had worked his way across the Atlantic on a cattle boat, later swearing he would never face a slice of beef or smell a rose ever again and Neville, a New Zealander who had shovelled coal as a stoker on a trampship and subsequently washed dishes in a restaurant in Soho, until the dogged perseverance of both was rewarded. I admired their courage in travelling so far with such faint hope but with the determination to get into the Royal Air Force and hold the King's Commission.

There was a South African, 'Kong', of Russian surname and extraction who appeared to limp, as if with a wooden leg, a handsome Irishman, Toby, with an Irish-Bronx accent, who believed it was more comfortable to lie down than sit, with a gleam in his eye that belied his apparent lethargy, two very tall languid Englishmen, one of whom obviously had much too much money and insufficient interest to last the course, and didn't, and the other, Denis, seemingly afflicted with a nervous eye tic, which virtually became a violent twitch under excitement.

We were at a loss to know how he had passed Medical Board until a little later when we discovered we were being 'sent up' by a master of the acting profession but at that time he was suffered gladly being an excellent pianist and delightful raconteur.

* * *

One evening we piled into our cars and headed for one of the locals for a quencher and on arrival, Denis, the Twitch, who had shown little interest in the conversation so far mumbled something about a walk in the fresh air, and disappeared.

Some time later the door opened and an old man shuffled up to the bar and Al, the Canadian, rather embarrassingly drew our attention to the old chap who was fumbling in an old purse and the pockets of his coat for three pence for his ale, producing eventually one penny, one halfpenny, another halfpenny and then nothing more and looking blankly, with embarrassment and shame, at the barman.

His bent shoulders, drooping lower in impecunious dejection, his long hair, matted, unkempt under a shapeless felt hat, his raincoat shabbily faded, torn, held by one button, his creaseless trousers slopping, frayed at the bottoms, over shoes worn down at sole and heel, unpolished for many a morn, touched us all. Al, though hearty, brash and loud, gently pushed aside the old man's hand, picked up the pathetic coins on the bar dropping them quickly into the purse saying softly, as he handed it to the man "I would be pleased if you would join me in a drink, old boy." (an expression he had adopted to Anglicise himself).

The old man, looked up at Al, held his gaze for a moment and said quietly, "Thank you, Sir, Your Good Health", picked up the glass of ale, his hand shaking and spilling beer down the old raincoat, as he raised it to his lips.

The fluffy haze of beer froth on the straggly moustache heightened the pathetic scene and we, in turn, hastened to buy the old boy a beer, brushing aside the tatty purse he still held and from which he had tried in vain to produce a miracle, the elusive extra one penny.

We had all, proudly and with varying degree of self-consciousness, patronised the old man who, after several rounds was now hanging on to the bar and chanting softly, more to himself than his audience and new-found friends of the evening, when it happened.

He took a large noisy gulp at his beer emptying the glass surprisingly without spilling a single drop, put down the glass and, in a metamorphosis so rapid that we must have stood staring with mouths agape for at least 15 seconds, swiftly straightened his bent back, removed his old felt hat, the unkempt hair falling away with it, the moustache ripping from his upper lip in a flash and his raincoat falling to the floor.

Denis stood there, his eyes glinting fiercely with the satisfaction of triumph and the delight and excitement of the faultless performance of an artiste and said gently in the croaky, querulous voice of the old man, "My turn now chaps, I believe."

The applause of stunned silence echoed through the smoky atmosphere of the bar, which must have been most gratifying to Denis, the erstwhile actor in the few seconds as the shock waves were lost in the air before we leapt at him, thumped him, doused him with beer hurling abuse that turned to screams of laughter as we all collapsed in a heap on the floor.

Denis had indeed scored a notable triumph, his days on the 'boards' it seemed, were not over. We were to be convulsed by a variety of hilarious performances in the months that followed during the happy days of flying training.

Chapter 2

8 FTS Montrose

Having completed the course on Tiger Moths without incident, although many fell by the wayside, and bade farewell to Perth, our depleted group reported in due course to RAF Montrose. Resplendent in brand new uniforms we were put through a concentrated two-term programme of flying and lectures that had us reeling in the effort to absorb and retain the knowledge that was poured at us without surcease. With the resilience of youth, we, in our eagerness, swallowed and digested everything like starving piranha fish and came back for more.

The new and exciting world of Service Life, with its protocol, discipline, Air Force Law, administration and the highly technical aspects of flying and navigating military aircraft encompassed us and the world outside had detached itself from our orbit.

During the first, or junior term, we all flew dual-control Hawker Hart biplanes and were given the same instruction in front gun, Lewis gun and bombing techniques, learning the strange art of night flying. In the second, or Senior term we were split into bomber (light, medium and heavy) and fighter units, mostly by choice, with a possibility of opting for a Squadron at the end of the term, if successfully completed.

We flew Harts, Hart Specials, Hinds, Demons and Audax fitted with Scarff rings and Lewis guns for air to air firing. I could not restrain my impatience to fly the Fury 1 biplane fighter which entranced me with the dainty, prancing walk of an Arab stallion, its staccato crackle from the stub exhausts and the feel of its very positive controls coming alive in one's hand as it climbed steeply into the sky. With guns mounted either side of the cowling firing through the arc of the propeller, the smell of hot machine oil and fabric dope, I was transported to flights of fancy, out-flying Richtofen, Ball, Mannock, McCudden, Bishop and all the other brilliant fighter aces in aerial combat over the Western Front in the 1st World War and in blissful ignorance of what the not too distant future held in store for me.

Apart from the dire necessity of cramming throughout the night for oral tests and written examinations our evenings were reasonably free, although we were inducted into the ceremonies of Dining-in and Guest Nights when, in immaculate mess kit we observed the niceties of Service protocol and discovered that a gentleman was not necessarily an officer and vice versa.

* * *

The highspot of Dining-in nights started with the relaxed atmosphere in the Ante-Room after dinner, before and during which, a piper of the Station Pipe Band had played in the Hall and who much later, puce in the face after a generous and surreptitious application of good whisky, was wont to burst the eardrums with cacophonous renderings of near-jazz, which, though applauded by us, left a look of stunned, unbelieving horror on the faces of the true Scots.

Station Pipe Band

Our instructors, superior beings who hardly deigned to acknowledge our existence under normal circumstance, would innocently suggest a game of high-cockolorum between a team of instructors and pupils. How easily and eagerly we took the bait. We were told to form a line, the first man with his back to the wall and the remaining five crouched hump-shouldered behind each other, the leading man with his arms about the waist of the first, or anchor-man and the rest, bent to the waist, holding the midriff of the man in front, forming in all a serpent of arched backs.

Six devils incarnate, transformed in a split second from what had been a moment before our patient instructors, would then in turn take a long run from the other end of the Ante-room, whooping like Red Indians, onto the backs of the unsuspecting pupils. The first man, the best sprinter would take the most prodigious leap to travel as far forward up the line as possible to leave room behind for the rest of the Comanches, soaring wildly in to the rafters before landing with a bone-shattering crunch on one of those below and hanging on with grim determination until all had leapt.

To be on the receiving end for the first time is indescribable – one expected a hard jolt and, braced one's legs and body firmly in anticipation as the pounding feet came nearer. But to receive a large, heavy, fit, hard-muscled screaming banshee on the head, neck, arms or small of the back can only be likened to the attack of a fully grown male lion from the uppermost branches of a large African tree.

But all is not over and worse may follow as the next tormentor may land on you also or fly over the top of his predecessor and touch down on the man in front, or bounce off and hit the floor at high speed. So no matter where you were in the line the suffering was intense and, until all the team had jumped, one stood like Atlas, bloody but unbowed. If flesh, blood, brain, sinews and muscles could stand no more, an ignominious collapse signified defeat, but to withstand the onslaught without giving way to a strong desire to die on the spot was gratifying in the applause of the onlookers and the anticipation of sweet revenge when, if one could ever straighten up again, the opportunity now arose to take one's revenge in inflicting similar or worse, retribution on one's tormentors.

It was all great fun and, although the death and casualty rate should have been appalling, only a few bruises, black eyes and torn mess kit were the total indications of battle and bloody mayhem that occurred in this and similar 'games-in-the-parlour' on Dining-in Nights.

* * *

At times, when the dual-control Hawker Harts were all in use, two trainee pilots would be instructed to take an Audax aircraft with one at the controls, the other in the rear gunners position, and carry out some minor exercise.

Being 'fighter' bent, this, on occasion, became a bit of a bind and one day Frankie, an irrepressible, diminutive and delightful character, and I, decided to liven the proceedings and bring a little warmth and light into the dull existence of the unlikeable and surly Flight Sergeant stationed at a desk in front of the hangar recording the busy aircraft movements.

The exhaust pipes on the Audax, one on either side of the fuselage, ran horizontally and could be used as a temporary foothold climbing in and out of the aircraft, having a heat shield on the upper surface.

Audax Light Bomber

We decided that we could, with a little care, having practised with the aircraft stationary on the ground, exchange seats in mid-air. By detaching and leaving our parachutes in the seats we were able to climb out of the cockpits, stand on the exhaust pipes, one to each side of the fuselage, leaving the aircraft to cope on its own for the time being, and which we grudgingly conceded it could, then shuffling as best we could in the slip-stream, the drag of which threatened to rip us from our precarious hold, to a position where we could climb in to the shelter of the cockpits.

All this took but a few seconds but seemed interminable. We were too worried to look down and very relieved when we had completed the foolhardy exchange.

As I had taken off and been duly recorded as pilot and Frankie as rear passenger, cum gunner, cum navigator, it must have come as a gentle surprise to the Flight Sergeant to see the Audax land and taxi past with Frankie up front at the controls and me sitting in the rear.

We saw him grab his pencil, make an alteration of his obvious mistake, and sit down, contented that his error had been rectified.

Frankie took off and again, at a suitable height and well clear of the airfield, we performed the aerial exchange which now we managed more easily.

Back we went to the airfield and I, up front, landed and taxied slowly past the Flight Sergeant who, this time, was getting hallucinations and last seen was scrubbing and scribbling madly at his desk.

Three's a lucky number, so I took off again and, once

more, we repeated the exchange of seats with a veritable scamper across the exhaust pipes.

Frankie brought the Audax in for its third landing and, as we grinned our way past the desk, the Flight Sergeant was a shattered man.

He wasn't exactly white-haired but had the haunted look of a man permitted visions but lacking the courage of belief.

Frankie and I climbed out of the Audax, well satisfied, and went over to the desk to sign the Authorisation Book on termination of the flight and I said, as casually as I could, without bursting into laughter, "Must have been a bit cold in the back all this time, we should have landed and swapped over."

The Flight Sergeant was muttering something to himself about "seeing the MO and getting glasses" as we walked into the hangar, but we never dared let on. We should have been sent to Hell for such a foolish and dangerous prank.

* * *

After a week's well earned leave at the end of our first term we returned to the Station to become the Senior Term, a mantle we assumed with appropriate dignity, and woe betide the junior term 'sprogs' who thought fit to associate with us on equal terms, as they were quickly disabused of their temerity and put firmly in their place from our pinnacle of seniority of three months. Pulling rank is a great pastime, even at the bottom of the ladder.

The remainder of the Course passed quickly. We enjoyed a brief spell on the East Coast at Catfoss, north east of Hull, where we carried out the practical applications of live air-to-air and air-to-ground attacks on targets in the Fury 1 biplane. We discovered with a great shock that what seemed so simple on paper in the lecture room was indeed a practical impossibility in a bucking fighter and we felt a much greater respect and admiration for those fighter aces of the 1914/18 War whose aircraft and equipment were by comparison most elementary, and we realised that we still had a lot to learn.

Fury I Fighter

Needless to say even this detachment to Catfoss was not without incident. Denis, 'the twitch', long overdue to enrich our lives with some quixotic or clottish performance, came up trumps with a simple exhibition of 'How to do the right thing the wrong way', or vice-versa.

He was detailed on a bombing exercise on the range, as bomb-aimer in a Hart or Audax and his aircraft was bombed up with practice smoke bombs on its racks and Denis was ensconced in the rear ready to prove to the RAF that its choice in him was not entirely misplaced. Little did they know that in Denis they had a winner but, on whose side, was the unspoken question.

* * *

The aircraft took off with a fellow pupil at the controls, normal procedure, and everything under control, one would have thought, forgetting that Denis was involved in the action, where anything could happen and, of course it did.

A pre-flight instruction to bomb-aimers was to ensure, before start up and take off and *before* the bombs had been fitted to the racks, that the bomb selector release mechanism worked satisfactorily, by the simple expedient of moving the bomb selector lever through its quadrant and back again, confirmed by the armourer below.

Needless to say, Denis, by some simple oversight, had forgotten this completely until the aircraft was airborne, and, in a flash, rectified his omission by shoving the selector lever fully forward to the 'all bombs gone position', satisfied that his attention to detail would not go unnoticed.

Unfortunately, the bombing range was some miles away so Denis' score was an absolute zero in the technical sense, yet startling in its effect.

A local farmer, peacefully and happily ploughing a few furrows in the field next to the airfield boundary never knew what hit him as Denis put down a plastering salvo of smoke bombs around him and his horse, which, taking a very poor view, promptly bolted.

I don't know who was the more red-faced when they met, the farmer from chasing his horse or Denis from sheer embarrassment, but, as no damage was done, the farmer was eventually persuaded by Denis to accept an invitation to dinner for he and his wife, which he generously accepted.

We suggested to Denis's embarrassed instructor that his unique form of 'blind-bombing' technique might well be adopted by the Service if Denis were given 'carte blanche' to train up bomber crews, but the instructor went terribly pale and tottered away muttering, "Oh God spare me, take me from pupil training and I'll be a good boy for ever, I promise."

* * *

I had not been in the least disturbed by, or would accept, the strong rumour circulating, that pilots with low passing-out grades were sent to Fighter Squadrons instead of Bomber units, with supposedly poor chances of future career promotion.

That I and a few others should actually opt to fly fighters was considered by our fellow pupils to be foolish in the extreme, but we had all set our target for the way ahead and nothing could deter us. In the event, in our opinion, we could not have made a better choice.

We crowded round the end of term postings on the Notice Board and I was overjoyed to find that my wish to join a Fighter Squadron had been granted.

Having said goodbye to my good friends of the previous

nine months who as I, had survived the slings and arrows of flying training, but of whom many would not survive the war on the distant horizon, I took a brief and very impatient leave before I could realise my ambition, that of becoming a member of a Royal Air Force Fighter Squadron and whose proud motto 'SEEK AND DESTROY' was, ere long, to be amply justified.

Wally, the 'Wingless Wonder'

CHAPTER 3

Fighter Squadron

I reported, with considerable trepidation, to my new Fighter Squadron Number 41 at Catterick in Yorkshire, very conscious of the brand new uniform I had obtained from Gieves, the tailors to the Services, with its, to me, glaring 'broad' stripes on its sleeves of a pilot officer and of which I was so proud. I entered an entirely new and fascinating world.

41 Squadron Spitfire I

The Squadron CO, Adjutant and pilots, both Officer and NCO accepted me with a pleasant, polite aloofness and I knew that, unless I could prove my worth, my probationary period would be very short.

I applied myself with even greater diligence, listening to every word, in Flight Office and Crew Room, that fell from the lips of my peers, who, although of my age, were fully trained fighter pilots, and whose bearing and actions carried an authority, decisiveness and dedication that I would be hard put to emulate.

They all lived and breathed 'fighters' and I wanted to share that air so badly I could hardly wait for the next day to begin.

My Flight Commander, a tall, dark, slim, young man, deceptively languid but one who brooked no carelessness, called me to his office and casually remarked, "You can take up a Fury on circuits and bumps and sector familiarisation for one hour and no more – you know the endurance, and don't get bloody lost." Waving an arm vaguely to his left, "The Pennines are there somewhere and the Clevelands are there", waving in the opposite direction, "So you shouldn't have any difficulty."

As I saluted and walked to the door he added, almost as an after thought, "But we always come home up the Great North Road or the Railway line if the weather closes in, it saves the bother of map reading."

I caught a glint in his eye, but dared not smile back. I was to learn later that he had done the long Navigation Course and there wasn't much he didn't know about getting safely from A to B, and back. The Fury II was as different from the untidy hack Fury I I had flown in training as a Rolls Royce is different to a Model T Ford.

* * *

Squadron Fury II Fighters 1938

I was excited as I climbed into the Fury, where the rigger, leaning over, helped me secure my harness straps. But, having started up, the familiar staccato crackle of the stub exhausts calmed me and I ran quickly through my cockpit check while the Kestrel warmed itself for take off.

Concentrating hard to avoid making a stupid mistake, aware that watchful eyes behind the hangar windows would not miss a single trick, I waved away the wheel chocks and taxied out.

The take off was a breathless moment, a dream, the Fury leaping forward as if possessed, wrapped tightly round me and almost taking the reins from me in its eagerness to climb up in to the Heavens.

As I cavorted about the sky, the Fury laid back its ears and ran like the wind and I felt an overwhelming gratitude that I had been granted something for which I would have given my eye teeth, or gladly done for nothing, but I was in some doubt how the Air Council would react if I offered them their money back, so I let that thought go.

The local landmarks were easy to identify but I knew that the squadron sector would have to be learnt by heart until one could dispense with maps, having instant recognition of the terrain below, to go to and return from any point without reference to course and track lines as one had learnt in training, and a lot of very hard work lay before me.

I returned to the airfield circuit, throttling back and bringing the Fury in on a tight turn close to the boundary and, side-slipping a little excess height, touched down.

The undercarriage of the Fury had oleo or compression legs that would forgive anything but extreme abuse, and on touch down the wheels, unlike Harts, Audax and Demons which, if not landed carefully would bound across the airfield in ever-increasing hops and jumps until something gave way, would stay glued firmly to the ground.

I reported back to the Flight Commander who commented: "Well, you didn't bend it then."

"No Sir" said I, "It knows its way in to this airfield better than I." And he smiled.

"Yes, it's a nice aircraft but has its limitations. We want more speed, more endurance and a lot more fire-power and one day we'll get a fighter with all these."

I don't know whether he was just being optimistic, or did he know that a genius named R.J. Mitchell was at that moment poring over his drawing boards at Eastleigh bringing to life a dream that would be a legend in its time, loved by those who flew it and putting the fear of God up those who opposed it?

* * *

The days, weeks and months passed in complete absorption as I learnt the finer arts of formation flying, battle climbs, tactics, camera-gun interception attacks on bomber aircraft and the thousand and one facets of life on a 'pukka' RAF Station, and my life was full.

My fellow pilots were a grand crowd, mainly British with four very Anglophile Canadians, whose enthusiasm never flagged and, once accepted, were only too pleased to assist me in my quest for knowledge and experience.

'Lulu', an Irishman, and Douglas, an Englishman who had incurred the dismay of his naval family at his decision to join the Junior and not the Senior Service, were flying with me in formation one day and, breaking in to line astern, we began a follow my leader round and round the lovely white persil-washed clouds.

Tearing round one cloud in a vertical turn with the stick well back, I could see Douglas hard on my heels but lost sight of 'Lulu' who should have been on Douglas' tail.

Halfway round the cloud's perimeter I heard a roar behind my head and caught a flash of a silver shape that, in a moment, passed between Douglas and I, missing us by inches.

The shape was a Fury with 'Lulu' at the helm travelling

at the same height and at right angles to our line of flight.

We eventually rejoined Vic formation and returned, somewhat subdued, at least two of us, to the airfield.

After landing Douglas and I walked over to 'Lulu's' aircraft and asked him what the hell he was playing at a while before.

"Oh," he drawled in his Irish brogue, "I had dropped a little behind you so I thought I'd take a short-cut to catch up!"

I looked at Douglas, he looked at me, our eyebrows rising to our hairline as we both remarked, "What can you do with a mad, bloody Irishman?"

And there's no answer to that, so we walked away.

* * *

The Deputy Flight Commander 'Cowboy' was responsible for part of the training programme, which continued without pause to improve and maintain the squadron at peak efficiency and no other air force could surpass the RAF in its zeal for perfection and which was to stand us in such good stead in Bomber, Fighter, Coastal and Training Commands when Hitler let slip his 'dogs of war'.

One pilot, 'Grannie', was apparently a little 'loose' in his formation flying and 'Cowboy' took him up in two Furies for a little formation practice to iron out the problem as his reaction and timing were not up to form.

The basic principle of formation flying is to stay steadily close at all times, on take off, climb, turn, approach and landing without 'waffling' from side to side or being too close or too far away, from excessive use of controls and throttle.

One had to ignore ones own attitude relative to the ground, concentrating entirely on keeping smoothly tucked in on the leader. If he took you into the deck it was very bad judgement on his part, and bloody bad luck for you.

The Fury aircraft had indifferent wheel brakes, operated on the rudder pedals by toe movement and it was normal practice on landing in formation for the lead aircraft in a 'Vic' of three to open up his throttle with a short burst, immediately after touch down, to pull himself clear of the formating aircraft and prevent any possibility of either aircraft swinging in from side wind effect and being unable to check the swing with brakes only.

Otherwise the propellers of formating aircraft could easily chew up the wings of the lead aircraft or more unpleasantly, the lead pilot might get 'a short back and sides' from the flailing airscrew.

'Cowboy' had impressed on 'Grannie' the necessity of staying very close and the take off and formation flying were, if not without criticism, carried out satisfactorily.

Without using radio we had a system of hand signals used by the leader to indicate various actions, open throttle, turn left or right, climb, dive, throttle back, etc. and 'Grannie' was alright until approach and touch down when 'Cowboy' signalled 'open throttle' meaning the throttle burst to pull him clear.

'Grannie' read this as open throttle for take off and opened up overtaking 'Cowboy' rapidly, who, to avoid becoming Fury mince, opened up again, whereupon

'Grannie' opened up once more. And so it went on.

'Cowboy' was chased up the airfield, signalling like mad with 'Grannie' hanging on like grim death, and 'Cowboy' trying desperately to lose him.

Eventually when 'Cowboy' decided that a rapid break-away from 'Grannie' was indicated and, using rudder, brakes and a throttle burst turned violently away from his tormentor, whereupon, to his horror, 'Grannie' not to be found wanting by not sticking to his leader, did likewise, like a new-born lamb after its mum, and probably bleating like it.

The farcical situation only ended with 'Cowboy' by this time perilously close to the hangars, waving his arms madly in a 'stop, switch off' signal and jumping out of his Fury, dancing up and down on the grass in exasperation and frustration.

The conversation that ensued does not bear repeating and is best forgotten, although 'Grannie' was heard to mutter, in a most aggrieved tone, that "After all, he did tell me to stay close."

Some learn the hard way, don't they?

* * *

About this time, in the Autumn of 1938, we were made aware that our dearly loved, but sadly obsolete, Fury 11's were to be replaced.

As Hurricanes were now re-equipping some Fighter Squadrons we were lifted to blissful heights of anticipation when we heard we were to be one of the first squadrons to be re-equipped with the new, sleek, very fast Spitfire monoplane fighters coming out of Supermarine, Eastleigh.

There appeared at Catterick a Magister monoplane which was replacing the old Tiger Moth for ab-initio training, a shaggy, second-hand Fairey Battle light bomber and a venerable Avro Tutor biplane which had also been used for years for elementary flying training, and was a delight to fly.

How we were to convert from slower single seat Fury II biplanes to very fast single seat Spitfire monoplanes, using these three as transitionals eluded us. I gave the Battle a very wide berth and avoided flying it and the Magister served no comparative purpose whatsoever. But everything has its use, not the least the old Tutor, so we had to devise means of making good use of what the Gods had placed before us.

There was a large, flattish field at Scorton adjacent to Catterick, and which later was to become an airfield, but at this time it was used for forced landing approach practice and, one day, 'Buck' and I took the Tutor for an airing and decided to practice forced landings on the Scorton field.

I suggested to 'Buck' that, to make life a little more interesting, we should have a small wager on each of us landing the Tutor from an agreed height and position after take off without use of engine power, the better to test our individual skills.

My fellow gambler agreed and I duly took off and, at the agreed moment, cut my throttle and proceeded with the business, as indeed it had become, of getting the Tutor round the perimeter of the field on the glide.

I turned in on overshoot, side-slipped the excess height

shortly before crossing the boundary hedge, fish-tailing and touching down quite easily, but the Tutor, like the Tiger Moth, could do a better job if left to its own devices so I claim no laurels for the attempt, but at least I was half a crown (2s. 6d.) old money, to the good, and that went a very long way in those days (5 pints of ale to be exact).

'Buck' was convinced that he would outsmart me and land in a shorter run from the boundary than I, which would give him the Win.

As he came round the perimeter of the field he was whistling and shouting, "Piece of cake, old boy, piece of cake. Get your half a crown ready – it's mine."

Not bloody likely, I thought, as he turned in to approach the boundary hedge, and, like I had, side-slipped the Tutor nonchalantly, straightened up and then, suddenly, realised too late that he had cut it too fine.

The boundary hedge loomed before not below us. Anticipating the low cunning of my friend, I had my left hand firmly on the throttle in the 'idle' position as I felt the insidious initial movement of the lever as 'Buck' tried to ease on a little power without, he thought, my being aware.

"You've had it, Buck, me old mate" I shouted down the mouthpiece still holding the throttle firmly back. "Give up, you've lost."

"Not bloody likely" said he, wrestling with the Tutor which, during this very brief hiatus, had packed in its hand.

We landed with a bump in the field next door, several feet short of the hedge and, as we bounced, I pushed the throttle wide open and we staggered over the hedge, and subsided in a bit of a flurry on the right side of the hedge.

We sat in the Tutor arguing on the unmoral, unethical attributes we both claimed the other possessed to the exclusion of all man made principles and decency until, in the mirror above me, I saw his eyes, and we both dissolved into howls of laughter.

"You're a dangerous bugger, aren't you when there's a bob on it?" said 'Buck'.

And I answered, politely but somewhat primly, "Far from being dangerous I just happen to think that elements of risk should be eliminated and I didn't think I should be flying today with a cheap, chiselling degenerate Welsher."

The argument raged with great humour as we flew back to Catterick and I was unrelaxed and ready for final retaliation, should it come, as we came in to land.

Sure enough, the throttle lever was nailed and boarded up in the idle position by 'Buck', grinning fiendishly at me in the mirror as he tried to play his last card.

I had built up sufficient extra air speed in the glide, which he hadn't noticed, to stretch it comfortably over the boundary and we touched down in silence.

"Ah, you're a cunning wicked little man" said 'Buck', shaking his head as we dismounted, and fumbling in his pocket for the half a crown I had won fairly, and rectangularly.

* * *

Late in the Autumn of 1938 the dreams we had nourished became reality when our first Spitfires arrived at our comparatively small grass airfield at Catterick. We gazed in awe at these beautiful, graceful yet menacing fighters that slid so effortlessly around the circuit, much faster than our Furies were capable of, with the deep-throated rumble of the mighty Merlin engines trailing in their wake.

The fuselages and wings were very ominous in their new brown and green camouflage colours, a presentiment of the shadow of things to come. This superb aircraft would write history across the skies of England when the German bomber and fighter crews would sound the alarm of 'Achtung - Schpitfeure'.

Squadron Spitfire I Fighters 1939

There had, at first, been doubts whether the Spitfire I, with its fixed very coarse pitch two-bladed wooden airscrew, could operate safely in and out of the small Catterick airfield, but we had no serious problems, and, later carried out night flying exercises with them. Eventually, we got a finer pitch airscrew which improved take off and climb but had its drawbacks at rated altitude and which was succeeded in 1939 by the three bladed 2-pitch airscrew.

There was no interim conversion from biplane to monoplane, Fury II to Spitfire I. We all had to take a brief written examination on familiarization and handling characteristics before being permitted to fly.

My turn came at last. I ran quickly through the start-up procedure, switched on, primed the engine, pressed the start button and, after a few rotations of the blades, the Merlin coughed into life, puffing a burst of smoke from its kidney exhausts as it settled down at fast tick-over. The cockpit check had to be rapid. The offset radiator meant the engine warmed up quickly and one must not hang about or coolant boiling would result before one could taxi out and take off.

Elevator trim set neutral, rudder bias trim set full right to help counteract the torque of the airscrew as the power of the Merlin was applied, hydraulic pressure up, undercarriage indicator lights on, radio check and clearance from control, fuel gauges, oil pressure, coolant temperature, flaps up, throttle-friction knob tight and a few minor incidentals and it was time to run up.

I throttled back, waved away the wheel chocks, and looking around quickly, opened the throttle, braking with the lever on the spade grip control column to swing the aircraft round towards the take-off point.

There was no runway and no airfield control caravan but a green Aldis lamp winked at me from the Watch Office as I swung the long nose of the Spitfire from side to side and I was in position for take off.

I tightened my harness, ran my eyes quickly over the instrument panel, not specifically observing what was correct and in order, but strangely aware that a faulty instrument reading would instantly attract my attention.

The throttle moved forward steadily under my left hand and the low rumble became a heavy thunder of sound, as the airscrew bit in to the air, the torque forcing the left wing down requiring heavy pressure on the right rudder to prevent the Spitfire from swinging off line.

Easing the control column forward the tail lifted and I had, at last, forward visibility over the long nose. Initial acceleration, after the Fury II, was disappointing with the coarse-bladed airscrew, but at 75 to 80 mph the Spitfire was ready to 'unstick'. I held it down on the ground a little longer then moved the control column gently back.

The wheels left the ground immediately and we were away in a fast shallow climb. Never before having flown an aircraft with retractable undercarriage and, recalling the handling drill, I transferred my left hand from the throttle to the control column and moving my right hand down by my side felt for, and found , the short lever to select wheels up. I moved the selector and then, moving my hand to the larger lever began to pump backwards and forwards and, as the pressure became firm saw the panel indicator light change to 'wheels up'.

Until one had flown the Spitfire a few times, and became accustomed to this pumping action, the natural reaction of the left arm was to move in the opposite direction as one pumped and the climbing Spitfire would undulate like a serpent until the motion was complete. Later Spitfires were equipped with fully automatic hydraulic motion on select and the porpoising and village pump work were eliminated.

Having raised the wheels I now moved my right hand above my head feeling for the canopy retaining catch and, releasing this quickly, slid the canopy forward to the closed position. The wind noise died away and I was in a rather hot capsule which, momentarily, seemed a little claustrophobic after open cockpits and I could hear the Rolls Royce Merlin singing 'basso profundo' in front of me.

After all this work down in the engine room, which only took a few moments I looked out to find the airfield boundary was far below and behind me and I throttled back to climbing boost pressure before I shot over the Pennines and out in to the Irish Sea.

The controls were now very firm but reasonably light though heavier than the Fury. I put on rudder and aileron into a left turn, levelling off at 2,000 feet, the movements of my hands and feet producing immediate and positive control, the airspeed indicator registering, unbelievably, well over 200 mph.

The thrill of the Tiger on first solo I had known, the thrill of the dainty Fury II I had known, but I was not prepared for a ride on a thoroughbred like this.

I flew around the Sector for 20 minutes arriving at recognition points so quickly that the earth appeared to have shrunk since I had taken off. Returning to the airfield circuit I throttled back but the Spitfire, being of such clean design was reluctant to slow down, unlike a biplane which with its excessive drag slowed quickly to circuit speed. For a long while afterwards we were all inclined to come rocketing into circuit at 200 mph or more.

I throttled back a little more to reduce speed to 140 mph on the down wind leg, selected 'wheels down' and pumped at the handle until I felt the wheels lock down and saw the panel indicator confirm.

The Spitfire with its much higher wing-loading could not

glide like a biplane and only later, with experience and better judgement, could one carry out a very tight circuit glide approach, fully throttled back, with wheels and flaps down.

Turning on to base leg I received a 'Green', clear to land, from the Watch Office Control and dropping the airspeed to about 120 mph slid open the canopy and selected flaps down. They operated only fully up or down, and my angle of approach steepened considerably.

It was advisable to come in on a close turn keeping the boundary in sight, as a long motored approach pitched the nose too high and reduced forward visibility to a minimum, and any aircraft taxiing for take off would be unsighted. Many accidents occurred with trainee pilots landing in this manner.

When I turned on to final approach I was much higher than I would have been in the Fury, but the Spitfire sank quickly and I sailed over the boundary at about 90 mph throttled right back, the nose rising to obscure forward vision as I eased the control column gently back.

I was quite unprepared for the float effect as the Spitfire held off the grass surface until, with a sigh of apparent resignation, it lost lift and touched down in a reasonable 3 point attitude, rolling up the airfield until checked gently with the brakes, which had to be used carefully or the Spitfire would easily tip up on its nose to one's great embarrassment.

As I taxied in towards the hangar I felt a warm sense of pleasure and excitement that I had flown the latest, fastest and finest fighter in the Royal Air Force and in the world and, although I subsequently flew many, many hours, in nearly every Mark of Spitfire that followed, I still vividly recall that momentous day.

* * *

Our day flying programme on the Spitfire progressed with little incident and early in 1939 we commenced night-flying. Again there was some doubt of night-flying Spitfire Mark I aircraft from our little grass airfield at Catterick but we carried out a full programme, not without a little heart-stopping but without incident, – well, almost!

We had not flown the Fury II biplane on night exercises due to the excessive, and blinding, flash back from the stub exhausts and the very brief flight endurance, so we were all rather rusty.

An old Demon biplane was produced by some well meaning magician and we did a few circuits and bumps for night familiarisation. I flew the thing one night and, happily wandering around Yorkshire, was suddenly brought up short by the noise of the engine which started to 'hunt' and vibrate like mad, and which, after a while faded out and ran normally. I thought – 'Oh no, there can't be two of these bloody voodoo kites' as I had night flown a Demon in training at Montrose which did this 'hunting' exhibition. Although frightening for a while it never packed up, but there's got to be a first time.

When I landed a little later I went to the crew room, took out my flying log book and sure enough it was the same dread Demon. No one else had this experience on this aircraft, but I gave it a very wide berth after that.

In those years night flying, at least on a Fighter station was, to say the least, a little unusual. The equipment composed of four items, a taxiing post (a Christmas tree effect intended to help one find the flare path), a Chance floodlight (also intended to help one find the ground) a flare path of six gooseneck paraffin flares (intended to keep one on the straight and narrow) and a remarkable angle of glide indicator (of which more later), and that was the lot. No beacons, no approach lights – nothing.

The equipment lay-out for night flying was the responsibility of the Duty Pilot and, hopefully, the duty roster provided a man of experience. But sometimes the flare path would be laid with remarkable and total disregard to wind direction and with the last flare virtually on the Great North Road, or on the tarmac in front of the hangar. Such touches could add considerable interest and zest to the programme.

The drill for take off was slightly Fred Karno. One started up on the tarmac and, after a brief cockpit and radio check, and clearance, taxied out as quickly as possible to avoid boiling up due to the offset radiator. Heading for the taxying post, one paused for a 'green' take off signal from the first flare, where a night flying controller held sway. Taxiing involved the continuous swinging of the nose of the Spitfire from side to side to see whether you were still on the airfield and where the hell you were going, half-blinded by the flames stabbing back from the kidney exhausts and looking for the No. 1 gooseneck flare, trying to avoid the glare from the Chance floodlight stationed to one side of the No. 1, supposedly giving a limited 'V' of light up the flare path but generally pointing anywhere but in that direction.

Having arrived, more by good fortune than preconceived intention, at the No. 1 flare without the nerves cracking completely, if a little frayed, you took position for take off. A quick look round the dimly lit office and it was all go. The two-bladed airscrew, chewing comparatively slowly and ineffectually made the apparent reluctance to get airborne disconcerting.

Roaring up the line of goosenecks one counted slowly up to six – the end of the line and the bloody thing was still chuntering merrily away and not 'unsticking' at all.

Eventually, a sweeping movement of the forearm and you were at least airborne approaching the Great North Road, low down, wheels down and the lights of passing cars a few feet below as you selected wheels up and pumped like mad until they were up and locked and you could close the canopy and settle to do whatever you had originally intended doing but had completely forgotten in the hectic moments of getting off the ground in one piece.

Beyond the Great North Road lay a large piggery and it was agreed that if you heard the pigs squealing their bloody heads off your take-off was a bit low.

Night formation flying of up to 12 aircraft, and simple interceptions in sections of three aircraft were carried out under full moon conditions above cloud. The experience was most exhilarating, keeping formation by relying solely on the port and starboard wing tip recognition lights to judge the formation distance. Night formation lost its attraction when Terry the Flight Commander insisted on ascending and descending through cloud in 'Vic' formation. That was not very amusing and could put years on you.

Landing by night was carried out if not with nonchalance and total unconcern, at least with a blend of resignation and panache. The Chance floodlight, so bright and glaring when on the ground, shone like a bicycle lamp as you came on the down and cross wind legs. Turning on to finals, after selecting wheels and flaps down, you searched downwards into the dark below for the angle of glide indicator, the angle of dangle, so called, stationed roughly in line with the flare path forward of the No. 1 flare, emitting a powerful light of about one candle power and generally only visible from a few yards. It shone a beam of light on three segments, the top, amber, indicating that you were above the glide path, the centre, green, on glide path and the lower, red below glide path. This worked admirably if one had the vision of a night hawk and the indicator had been set up properly but, generally it was pre-set for high-flying balloons or submarines or some bloody fool stood in front of it at the wrong moment or some other bloody fool decided that the adjustment needed a twirl and wrecked the settings.

Then the fun would begin and the night exercise took on a less sombre atmosphere with pilots, on green, holding off at the No. 1 flare and sailing merrily up the flare path until realising that the airfield surface could not get up any higher, finally opening up and going round again to a blast of abuse on the R/T.

Conversely, and less amusing, approaching on green, coming in much too low and collecting, as Pooky did, most of the upper foliage of a clump of trees on the airfield boundary, which on every night flying exercise was always aligned with the flare path with unnerving accuracy.

One was against hurting the feeling of the hard working

personnel operating the equipment, who might in a fit of churlish pique, douse all the lights and go home, but it was found that sensible use of the downward landing light fitted to the Spitfire was of great value in judging final approach and which practice was to be a God-send to me at a later date.

With the advent of runways, static lighting, beams, markers, approach lights, etc., and the 1,001 aids to night flying that soon followed, our equipment by comparison was starkly elementary but at least one learnt, albeit the hard way.

* * *

It has always been mandatory in the Services that the protocol of seniority, even in the same rank by a short period, should be strictly observed. But one officer, senior to me by 12 months in the Squadron, was at times rather overbearing and irritating in the expounding of greater knowledge and experience. He was constantly reiterating the necessity of always making sure that nothing was ever overlooked or left to chance.

Such admirable traits were spoilt by his attitude of superiority, the impression created that he alone possessed all the necessary attributes and virtues and that we, the common herd, were just poor, ignorant, misguided 'Sprogs' to be suffered for their mistakes.

One night, the exercise to be carried out had to be done as an individual operation and, taking place directly over the airfield, would be watched, with critical eye by everyone else.

The Spitfire was fitted with a parachute flare and the pilot would take off by normal aids and fly away on a heading for several minutes and then call for a 'Homing' bearing back to base. He would be 'vectored', or guided back, by bearings, to the airfield, which was now unlit by any form of night flying aids such as flare path or floodlight, and in complete darkness.

On receiving a reciprocal bearing from those given to bring him back to base, which indicated that, in the darkness he had passed over the airfield he would turn very rapidly through 180 degrees estimating by his rate of turn his position to bring him back directly over the airfield. He would then 'poop off' his parachute flare, hopefully by his dead reckoning and judgement, directly over the airfield and then he would proceed to land by its light as it swung back and forth.

It was a difficult and demanding exercise which certainly put us on our mettle and we all did reasonably well, the evening proceeding with some exciting incidents as pilots 'pooped off' too early, too late or too low and scrambled into the airfield with the flare almost down to earth.

Our friend duly took off and climbed into the night and a little later we heard the Spitfire approach and pass over, turning quickly back on reciprocal course for the airfield. The sudden burst of brilliant light, as the flare was dropped, illuminated the airfield clearly and it was the best of the lot, floating down gently over the exact centre.

The pilot switched on his aircraft recognition lights and all our eyes followed him round the circuit as he turned quickly on to final approach. It was odd that no-one noticed, until too late, when a belated red warning Verey light shot up into the night sky as the Spitfire came in to hold off perfectly under the flare, that he had made the cardinal 'boob' and forgotten to lower his undercarriage, despite the audible and visual warnings or had deliberately cut the warning switch throttled back and forgotten, in the excitement, to check his panel lights.

The Spitfire sank lower and lower and, as lift expired and gravity took over, the blades of the airscrew snapped against the earth and the fuselage slithered and slithered on its belly for some distance and gradually slowed to a stop.

The parachute flare still hung tantalisingly in its brilliance above the pilot's head as he sat in shocked dismay in the cockpit and, watching, we felt sympathy for a man whose bubble of the search for infallibility had burst open upon him like the all revealing flare above.

It is so easy to be wise after the event but, realising that 'there, but for the grace of God, go I', we held our silence. This incident changed our friend who subsequently became very human, and understanding and modestly helped us along the road to perfection and on which he had momentarily stumbled.

He left the Squadron shortly after the outbreak of War and had a brilliant record in the hectic days of 1940 but, like a lot of our friends, was eventually killed in action.

* * *

One evening in April 1939 the Met. Office had forecast good visibility and conditions for a cross-country flight from Catterick to Digby in Lincolnshire, to refuel and return. I had no qualms of landing and taking off from a strange airfield at night as we had been flying the Spitfires for several months and were well advanced in our night-flying programme.

Hunched in the cockpit of the Spitfire, I gave the fitter, seen dimly over the top of the wing, the signal to start up and, as he bent to the button on his 'trolly-acc' plugged into the fuselage, I primed the engine, set the mixture control and throttle setting, switched on the magnetos and pressed the starter button.

The Merlin engine whirred, the airscrew revolving slowly, and spluttering, coughing and gouting flame and smoke, burst into rumbling life. While the fitter removed the umbilical plug I checked over the cockpit, letting the engine warm up in fast tick over. All instruments were reading correctly so, turning down the instrument panel rheostat until a faint glow gave sufficient light to read the panel clearly I looked out and up into the night sky.

Satisfied, relaxed and yet unconsciously tensed, I waved my hands above my head for the wheel chocks to be removed and, pushing forward the throttle, wheeled the aircraft in the direction of the taxying post and flare path.

Right on time I cleared Control on the R/T at No. 1 Flare, opened the throttle, the Spitfire dipping its wing with the torque as it accelerated, gathered speed rapidly and with a little help from me, climbed steeply into the night.

At 3000 feet over the airfield I set course southwards and settled down to the business in hand, warm and reasonably cosy in my little compartment, the Merlin humming gently to itself, and listening to the faint chatter of aircraft taking off from base at intervals behind me.

The landmarks on my track were coming up well, the lights of Northallerton, Thirsk and the brighter glare of York over to my left and the Rivers Ouse and Trent in the Estuary of the Humber gleaming in the pale moonlight.

Doncaster's lights way over to my right had disappeared and I was searching for the lights of Lincoln when the cloud formations built up heavily ahead. I lost height to keep below them, running in to heavy rain beating on my windscreen and canopy and visibility deteriorating rapidly.

I had switched radio channels and called Digby control but, after several calls, static background noise obliterated everything and eliminated all possibility of contact. I realised that I was not going to get in to Digby that night.

I had seen no airfield carrying out night-flying on my way down and, in any case, without radio contacts, decided to return to base rather than thrash around all night looking for shelter.

Turning the Spitfire on to a reciprocal course I headed back home trusting that the weather had not closed down there as rapidly as it had near Digby and which now covered my return track.

The pleasure had gone now, and I was blissfully unaware that a recall had gone out at Catterick as the storms moved in eastwards over the Pennines with unexpected speed. I had been beyond radio range and there I was, little orphan Annie out in the bloody rain and darkness and wondering if I should have to get out and walk before long.

I was now flying in very heavy rain just below the low, menacing storm clouds, not unduly worried, as no high ground existed for the time being and believing that the weather would clear as I went further North. But it was painfully obvious that I was in the middle of a particularly unpleasant frontal system.

Having of necessity dropped lower to 300 feet, with my landing light on, canopy open, searching urgently for landmarks, the adrenalin pumping quite a bit now, I caught a reflection of water and lights and hoped my quick appraisal was correct and I had passed over Goole on the River Ouse.

The Hull – Selby railway line flashed below and in the time it took me to kick on hard left rudder and aileron I had weighed up my chances of getting back to Catterick in such conditions and discarded all as quickly, knowing the odds were against me.

If I climbed up into and above the forbidding clouds to get a radio bearing I had no assurance, with the HF radio sets we had then that I would make contact for a bearing, with the static crackling in my earphones, and then I couldn't let down again through that lot without the probability of striking high ground, the Pennines to the West or the Clevelands to the right. If I stayed low all the way I stood an excellent chance of ploughing into something, flying as I was at submarine level. I had no intention of baling out and losing my lovely 'P' for Peter, still muttering gently to itself and oblivious of the storm without and the turmoil within.

I knew as I straightened up that I had made the right decision, the railway lines glistening in my landing light as it led me over Selby to the triangle of lines close to the small old airfield of Sherburn in Elmet, and, swinging very hard right, I knew the line north to York would in a few moments take me to the verge of the airfield boundary of

RAF Church Fenton. As I kept the line on my left the western airfield boundary flashed under my starboard wing.

In the lashing rain I swung hard right and left again into a tight circuit of the airfield, ominously dark, with only the lights of the Messes and Quarters blinking below. I couldn't help grinning to myself, imagining the look on the faces below as I roared over their roofs, and their indignation at being so rudely disturbed over their ale – and how I could do with one just now.

Screeching, unheard "Wakey, Wakey, you dozey buggers, let's have a little of that famous Northern hospitality and a fatted calf, or a ham sandwich," I circled several times still very low, flashing morse signals on my downward recognition light with touching pleas for a flare-path, or a ladder, supper, ale, a cigarette, bed and breakfast and any other stupid thing I could think of to pass the time – after all, I had nothing better to do. But no one seemed particularly interested and I waited with restrained impatience for someone to lay on a few flares and a floodlight until, prompted to check my instruments, I realised time was now very much of the essence as, pressing my fuel gauge button I found my tanks were emptying fast.

Lights were now flickering around the Watch Office and I felt sorry for the men who had been pressed into action to help me in the torrential rain, but I could wait no longer and, dropping my undercarriage, did a slow run low down hoping they would get the message that I was coming in, regardless.

Landing a Spitfire by night with the existent facilities of base was no easy matter and to attempt it with no aids, in low cloud and heavy rain conditions, on a strange airfield, presented problems I must now resolve.

The procedure in itself was simple. The first attempt must be the only one, fuel shortage dictated this. If I came in too low I might hit an unseen obstruction on the approach. If too high, I should touch down too far up the airfield and probably hit the far boundary.

The westerly wind was very strong and I came down wind just outside the south boundary, lowering my undercart and tightening my harness till it hurt, going very fast but not prepared to lose speed as I knew I must soon turn very sharply, very quickly, very low down, and I did not intend to stall and spin in on the last leg.

The down wind boundary shot under my port wing and I counted slowly and deliberately, yet horribly uncertain, before turning hard to port, rate four, straightening up blindly, turning port rate four again into wind, offering up a quick prayer before throttling back and quickly flipping the flaps selector to 'DOWN'.

I was committed – I had decided I must overshoot slightly and side-slip in for better visibility and jammed on right rudder regardless, feeling the wind and rain blinding in to the port side of the open canopy and sensed rather than saw the hedges pass below the wheels.

I kicked hard left rudder until the Spitfire swung straight and lined up for touch down.

The grass surface was a wet dark blur and I couldn't judge my height and had the horrible feeling that the aircraft would drop from my hands.

A quick burst of throttle and I caught it as it settled and before I knew it the Spitfire had put me down with hardly a bump, and rolled up the airfield in total darkness.

I felt the tension drain away as I taxied up to the welcoming lights of the Watch Office, braked and switched off the engine and fuel controls, sitting for a moment in silent gratitude.

Removed my soaked leather helmet and oxygen mask I held up my wet, sweaty face to the cool rain, still sheeting down, and sizzling and spitting on the hot exhaust stubs, and climbed slowly from the cockpit.

As I closed the canopy and stepped down to the grass I fondly patted the flank of 'P' for Peter, thinking 'If the bar's closed I am sure I shall go bloody mad.'

Apparently, the unexpected storm conditions that evening played havoc with other night-flying exercises in the country and one or two aircraft were lost and the pilots missing, with several others crashing on landing in the foul weather.

I flew back to Catterick the following morning and was told to report to the CO's office, where he sat with my Flight Commander.

"We managed to recall all the aircraft behind you, but you were out of range and Digby heard your first call but couldn't make contact. Thought we had lost you until you rang and said you had landed at Church Fenton. To land a Spitfire at night on a strange unlit airfield in storm conditions takes a bit of doing. I am very proud of you and pleased that you are with 41 Squadron."

The Flight Commander was watching me intently and I flushed as I caught the gleam of agreement in his eyes.

* * *

Some time after the release of news of the introduction of the Spitfire into Squadron service we were informed that the BBC would be visiting the squadron to prepare a radio programme about the new fighter and its pilots.

In due course a convoy of BBC vehicles arrived with a posse of rather supercilious types who, when deigning to speak to anyone below the rank of Squadron Leader, gave orders for their requirements in a manner that, to say the least, was damnably rude. We suffered the indignity and co-operated as best we could, reducing the abbreviation BBC to 'Bumptious Bloody Clots'.

I was called to the CO's office and instructed to put up a Spitfire in the firing position on the butts, a sand-filled enclosure where live ammunition could be fired to test the eight Browning guns mounted in the wings of the aircraft. I was to give a demonstration of the fire-power for recording.

The Spitfire was made ready and the BBC trundled a recording vehicle to within a few feet of the butts and the chap in charge told me to proceed. I was a little piqued at this peremptory order but, being the meek little fellow I am, proceeded.

As I climbed into the cockpit and put on my helmet I felt I must be fair, so I leaned out and suggested to him that it might be a good idea to stand a little further away to make his commentary and sound effect but he took as much notice as if I had impolitely suggested that the microphone be stuck in his ear, or elsewhere, and waved me on. I could see the armourers, thumbs-up, grinning in fiendish anticipation and I pressed the 'Fire' button with a faint touch of venom.

The cacophony of noise that erupts when eight very quick-firing Browning guns open up in unison, like rapid tearing of chain metal was, in the confines of the butts, completely shattering.

The BBC bird, a shocked look on his face, dropped his microphone and ran. Meanwhile his unfortunate assistant in the vehicle, twiddling the volume controls, was assailed in his earphones by this terrific din and came charging out, clutching his ears and shouting, "Jeeesus Christ, the bloody set's on fire and I'm bloody deaf."

He wasn't hurt, a blow more to his dignity than his ear-drums, but he couldn't hear anyone asking him to have a drink in the Mess for a long while that evening. The other BBC man, with the big mouth and microphone was most upset, and used naughty words, when I suggested that he might like to come a little closer for another short serenade on the Browning piano for luck. No matter how you try you just cannot please some people, can you?

* * *

Some days nothing happens to raise a laugh and one morning, after an exercise that would not go right we landed and walked, not very happily, into the crew room.

From the Flight Commander's office window the sound of hysterical laughter prompted us to look in. "Come in chaps," he called, "and listen to this, because I just cannot believe it."

It appeared that a very recent replacement, a Sergeant Pilot had taken off shortly before us with instructions to practice slow rolls for an hour. After two hours, he had not landed back at base.

Before 'overdue' action could be taken the Flight Commander had received a telephone call and on to the line came the Sergeant Pilot who, quite matter of factly, reported that he had landed to refuel, and would return shortly.

"But where the hell are you?" was the quite reasonable question from the Flight Commander.

"In Norfolk, Sir," came the reply.

He had slow rolled and slow rolled again all the way from Yorkshire, down over the Wash to the coast of Norfolk near Great Yarmouth before deciding to call it a day.

It was indeed unbelievable and too good to be true.

The Flight Commander's cold voice on the telephone disabused the pilot of thoughts of a future in our Squadron. He said, "Refuel your aircraft and fly it back here at once, right side up, and, when you have landed, go to your room pack your bags and be prepared to roll yourself right off this station, you are most certainly surplus to our requirements". The telephone clicked dead, as dead as the career of the fool on the other end of the line.

* * *

Terry, a very keen, experienced pilot had become Flight Commander and we (Terry, Lulu and I) had practised high-speed dives with an accelerometer fitted to each aircraft that indicated maximum 'G', or gravity, force on pull out of the dive. After we had pushed our 'G' threshold (conscious condition before black-out) sufficiently we took off for a pukka test run, climbing in loose Vic formation to just over 30,000 feet, the sky clear and ideal for our purpose.

On a signal from Terry we half-rolled together on to our backs, pulled back our control columns in unison and, trimming forward on the elevator trims, with throttles wide open, commenced a vertical dive.

The intention of the exercise was to put our Spitfires into terminal velocity dives to discover whether over-revving of the Merlin engine would, under such conditions, result in engine overstress and breakdown or disintegration.

Within seconds the airspeed indicators were going clockwise round the dials like mad and the altimeters were unwinding in the opposite direction, peeling off hundreds of feet per second as the earth rushed up to meet us.

Passing 10,000 feet Terry signalled 'throttle back' and began to pull out. His Spitfire and Lulu's were emitting smoke, as I imagined, mine was too, but the immediate problem was control. The control column, elevators and rudder had become virtually solid, immovable, with heavy buffeting and vibrations shaking the aircraft and indications of control reversal.

After what seemed an interminable time we were able, by pulling back on the control column with all our strength and applying gentle backward movement of the elevator trim, to gradually flatten out the headlong dive but it was impossible to use rudder or aileron movement for some time as we levelled off at about 2,000 feet.

By this time Terry's Spitfire was pouring out heavy smoke as it packed up under the strain. Lulu and I were still on power and followed Terry closely as he switched off his engine and, with ample time to drop his undercart and flaps, made a beautiful dead-stick landing on the airfield.

By the time Lulu and I had landed and taxied onto the tarmac the fire tender and crew were at Terry's Spitfire and an incipient fire outbreak was quickly subdued.

We had not previously dived the Spitfires to such extreme and were feeling the strain a little, unaware that we had in fact been 'tanking on' at near 600 miles per hour in the terminal velocity dive.

The exercise apparently produced some useful information for Rolls Royce and Supermarine, ever intent on improvement to engine and airframe.

* * *

It was nearly time for lunch and walking together to the Mess a voice called me from a window of sick quarters. It was the Station Medical Officer Dickie S –

Stepping inside, I knocked at Dickie's door and walked in. "I've been checking your Squadron jabs and you are way overdue," said he, "We'll do it now, it won't take a moment."

"Not on your bloody nellie" said I, ever polite and courteous, and headed rapidly for the open window, managing to get my head and shoulders out before Dickie made a grab for my legs and heaved backwards.

In those days battledress had not been introduced and, overalls being too hot to wear in a Spitfire except at high altitude, we chose to fly in uniform and, inevitably, excessive wear in the trouser seat and elbows necessitated a re-panelling operation at the camp tailors to extend the flying life of the garment.

My old uniform had had the treatment but old wine into new glasses or vice-versa my trousers wouldn't stand the strain of Dickie swinging like Tarzan from my legs and, with an ominous rending noise, the new patches parted company with the old.

Dickie howled with laughter as, rearwards I was exposed to the elements and, in a spirit of appeasement and negotiation, offered to lend me a pair of trousers if I would agree to the jabs.

With all the dignity a torn posterior would permit I scorned his offer and scrambled out on to the path outside.

I quickly found that, by leaning backwards at an acute angle I could manage to reduce the gaping and draughty hole at the rear so I stepped on to the road and headed at an oblique angle for the Mess.

Unfortunately the road took me immediately past Station Headquarters and who should at that moment step out from his office but the Station Commander Guy Carter. He was a capital, charming man and had a soft spot for us having been in our Squadron in the 14/18 War.

"Good morning," he greeted me and stepped out smartly towards the Mess.

I saluted as best I could, mumbled "Good morning, Sir," and attempted to keep pace with him, but walking at 45 degrees is virtually impossible and must attract the attention of any but the blind and the C.O. was quick to notice my weird progress.

"Hurt your back?" he enquired.

"Yes Sir, just a slight bruise."

"You should see the M.O. get some treatment" he remarked.

"I've just had the treatment Sir," I said with conviction and feeling.

Conversation faded to trivialities as I held the hall door open for the C.O. to enter and behind me the voice of Dickie "You didn't fool the old man you know," he said with glee. "He was watching from his office as you went through my window and was laughing like a drain."

Over a beer in the ante-room after I had changed my uniform the Station Commander remarked with a flicker in his eye as I stood upright once more. "Dickie's a good M.O., seems to have cured you in no time."

"Yes Sir" said I, thinking that I must find an alternative route between the hangars and the Mess until Dickie had, I hoped, forgotten about my jabs.

Chapter 4

The War Years

It was August 1939 and the foul seeds of War, sown by the Nazis, were now blossoming and being carried to us on ominous winds. The news of the build-up of their military strength could only herald the inevitability of major conflict in Europe.

A year earlier, at the Munich Crisis, when the country's fighter defence was composed of only a few squadrons of slow obsolete Gloster Gladiators, Gauntlets and Hawker Fury biplane fighters, we had been pitifully equipped to resist any major aggression. The Germans, even then, were capable but not yet ready to strike until they had built up an overwhelming preponderance of fast monoplane bombers and fighters. History books relate the circumstances of the 1938 Crisis when Britain obtained a precious and brief breathing space in which to face the future.

Although the German aircraft factories were producing a prodigious number of bombers – Heinkel, Dornier and Junkers, and Messerschmidt was turning out the ME 109 and 110 fighters in vast quantities on a mass-production basis, our own brilliant 'boffins' had been quietly at work also on the design of new fighters. The remarkable genius of Sidney Camm at Hawkers produced the Hurricane and R.J. Mitchell at Supermarine, the Spitfire.

The Hurricanes came into squadron service first, followed in the summer of 1938 by the Spitfires in much smaller quantities. Fighter Command under the genius of Air Marshal 'Stuffy' Dowding made full use of the time available to re-equip and train pilots to the new, fast fighter concept.

41(F) Squadron at Catterick had been fortunate to re-equip with some of the first Spitfires in the Autumn of 1938. We were soon fully operational by day and night and, as the months passed, our aircraft were modified and improved considerably, with increased boost pressure, and engine power, three-bladed variable pitch airscrews, new reflector gunsights, armoured windscreens, domed canopies, head and body armour and increased ammunition capacity for the guns.

We were getting on the top line, we had the best fighters, though small in number, we had the best pilots, highly trained and dedicated, the best leaders, in whom we had explicit trust, and the will and determination to resist aggression. Knowing we should be out-numbered, we were apprehensive, but waited with a remarkable calmness and confidence that would not be shaken.

Fighter command tactics had long been laid down, to which we should rigidly adhere, but in the early months of 1939 we had made many practice interceptions on bomber and fighter aircraft and were convinced, even then, that some of the tactics were now inoperable. Although not daring to raise a voice in criticism, we carried out our own modified tactics in formation approach and attack in our practices.

The powers that be were aware of the rumbles of

dissension from many fighter squadrons but it was left until actual combat occurred before any official changes would even be considered. The hectic air fighting around Dunkirk during the evacuation of the BEF in May and June 1940 provided ample evidence of the necessity for change and the more discerning fighter pilots were quick to adapt to more flexible formations for interception and attack. The success of their tactics became very apparent yet Fighter Command provided no immediate directive to change from the hitherto rigid, inflexible principles laid down.

The Squadron had been dispersed to camouflaged positions on the airfield perimeter well before the 3 September 1939. Being on day and night readiness, we were crudely established in bell tents with no creature comforts, but were permitted to go across the airfield to the Mess for meals, and slept on hard cot beds at dispersal in great discomfort.

Squadron pilots September 1939

The first day of War passed, unexpectedly, without event and my first 'scramble' of the War occurred on the night of the 4 September when two of us went up in the black-out in a vain search for a reconnaissance aircraft, far out into the North Sea. We were 'scrambled' by day often, generally in sections of three Spitfires, tearing over the Cleveland Hills to the coast and out to sea, chasing 'bogies', high-flying recce aircraft that had been radar-traced crossing the 'action line', some 80 miles out into the North Sea, but which had departed for Hitler, home and bed long before we got there. At least it sharpened up our take-off time, a maximum of three minutes, which we reduced to two or less with practice.

The drill for 'scramble' was simplicity itself, yet often, in those early days, reduced to a bloody shambles by over-excitement and anticipation.

The two flights of the Squadron took turns at Readiness, the other being at 15 minute stand-by, unless the Squadron was alerted, when all hell would probably break loose.

Generally, two sections of three pilots would be playing cards, or sleeping off the night before, when the telephone from the OPS Room would ring 'Scramble, Blue Section'. Before the telephone could be replaced, three pilots, already wearing Mae Wests, would charge through the tent flap, flattening all before them, running now like hares, with the ground crew, also alerted, for their aircraft. A leap for the wing, a leg-over into the cockpit seat and, as the rigger dropped the top parachute straps over each shoulder, the pilot would, in a flash, in a movement smooth with practice, with the eight hands of an octopus simultaneously switch on petrol cocks, prime the engine (if required) put on his helmet, plug in and switch on radio, call Control for instructions, (ie height, vector, and trade), check the airscrew pitch control and trimming tabs, lock his harness, switch on and with a signal to the airman at the trolley-acc. to press his button, and start-up. As the engine fired, a signal to remove the chocks in front of the wheels and the leader would open his throttle and surge forward. The engines of the aircraft at Readiness were always kept warm so without delay, the two support aircraft close alongside, (and woe betide the laggard) the section would swing out of the dispersal bay and with a deafening crescendo of noise, regardless of wind direction, tear straight across the airfield at full gallop.

Lifting off, the leader still exchanging pleasantries with Control on radio, the undercarriages of the three Spitfires would retract simultaneously the moment the wheels left the ground. The No. 2 and No. 3 aircraft would close up tight and the section would bank over vertically in a very tight turn for the right heading and climb steeply and disappear, leaving a remarkable silence as if the frenzy of a few moments before had just been imagined.

During this period of 'hard-lying', or roughing it in tents, the station equipment officer had been persuaded that, under Section ABC, sub-section XYZ of some regulation or other, we were entitled to a rum ration each day. Our Flight Sergeant in charge of the ground crews, a grand regular of the old school knowing King's Regulations by heart, backwards, was instrumental in obtaining the rum and, on the first day of issue lined up the airmen with their tin mugs at the ready. He knew that the issue rum had been in the stores for years and was possessed of vintage, lethal potency.

"Now this 'ere rum ain't the mother's milk wot you swill

down when you're out on the ran-tan", says he. "This 'ere's for men not bloody children, like you lot, so be careful and treat it with some bloody respect". He started to ladle it out.

One airman took a sniff of the potion and after a quick sip said to his mates, "Christ, it's weaker than horse-piss", a comment that required no contradiction in terms, and quaffed his ration in one gulp.

His eyeballs rotated up under his eye lids, his face turned puce, he gasped with a massive intake of breath and went down backwards, out like a light, stoned, literally, to the eyeballs.

The Flight Sergeant rapped out a command to the other airmen "Pick the dozey bugger up and take him out of my bloody sight, I hate good stuff going to waste" and turned to me, remarking with a fiendish grin "You know, Sir, I ought to be a bloody qualified nurse not a technical NCO. I can't tell these kids anything – in one ear and out the other bugger," and walked away with his rum jar, still mumbling to himself.

A few nights later 'Cowboy' and I were doing the two-pilot readiness, sitting in our tent, reading, sensibly wearing our pyjamas in the hot, airless atmosphere, heated by a large paraffin stove and lit by a large oil-lamp, able in a flash to pull on trousers, tunic and Mae West before rushing out to our aircraft if there was a 'scramble'.

The Flight Sergeant came in and, with a perfectly straight face, quite unnecessarily apologised for making an error in drawing the day's rum ration, of which there was, he said, a slight surplus, and which, to my untutored eye, seemed like a hell of a lot of lotion. He innocently enquired if we would care to join him in a tot before it went of and we adjourned to his tent.

If our quarters were hot and stuffy, the Flight Sergeant's tent, by comparison, was a blast-furnace that took one's breath away but, making no comment, we became seated and 'Cowboy', after a couple of sips of the elixir removed his pyjama jacket to try to keep a little cooler. Of course, the Ops bell rang for a single aircraft 'scramble'.

Normally, on these night 'scrambles' one would be up for 20 minutes or so at about 5,000 feet before a 'pancake', the recall to return to base. As 'Cowboy' charged out to his Spitfire, just in his pyjama trousers and Mae West, he shouted to me, "Don't drink my bloody rum, I'll be back in a few minutes" and quickly became airborne.

The cockpit of a Spitfire was an over-warm office up to a few thousand feet, after which it became progressively cooler with altitude until brass monkeys were tapping on the canopy. It wasn't 'Cowboy's' night, he'd pulled the short straw. Control sent him up to 15,000 feet and held him there for over an hour, dressed more for a sun-bathing jaunt than an arctic expedition.

When the Spitfire eventually landed, a shaking, shivering half-naked, frozen figure was prised from the cockpit and, staggering to the tent, a very shattered 'Cowboy' gladly accepted and drank a large tot of rum from the Flight Sergeant and we slowly defrosted him before the red-hot stove.

"Do you know," he said, without rancour, but in a somewhat disgruntled voice, "I called Control after half an hour and told them I was in my pyjama trousers and freezing and all bloody 'Bully' (the Controller) could say was 'Stay where you are, old boy, I'll bring you up a nice cup of Ovaltine and tuck you in'." "That's the trouble with you English" continued 'Cowboy' philosophically, holding out his empty glass to the Flight Sergeant for more nourishment. "No sympathy, no bloody sympathy, cold-hearted bastards. That bloody 'Bully' just sat down there in the warm Ops room singing to me up there 'We are the Ovaltineys, little girls and boys' (the old Ovaltine radio chant) and laughing his bloody head off."

* * *

At this time, two remarkable characters arrived on the Station, one being the incomparable Richard 'Batchy' Atcherley, formerly one of the team of brilliant pilots who in 1931 established the World Speed Record in excess of 400 miles per hour in the Supermarine S6 floatplane and which also captured the Schneider Trophy outright for Britain. R.J. Mitchell, the 'father' of the Spitfire designed the S6B and made full use of much of the design work to be incorporated eventually into the Spitfire concept.

'Batchy' had been posted to Catterick to train up 219 Squadron as one of the first night fighter defence units on Blenheims. Hurricanes and Spitfires had carried out the interim role but were limited in range and equipment, and to perform day and night readiness was putting a strain on the pilots. In addition a twin-engined aircraft would be able to carry specialised airborne radar detection equipment which was being developed and would, with its highly trained operators, ere long cause havoc amongst the marauding German bombers.

'Batchy' arrived at dusk one very dark and rainy Saturday evening and promptly borrowed a small communications low-wing four seater monoplane, used by 26 Army Co-operation Squadron, who were still sharing the airfield with us. He calmly proceeded, without the use of a flare path, Chance light, or other aids, to practice night flying circuits and bumps until the hedge bordering the Great North Road ran into him in the dark, so he called it a day, and packed it in for the night.

Although a tee-totaller, he had a wonderful flair for starting the most hilarious impromptu Mess parties in which we joined with wary gusto. To say that these occasions were trials of strength and endurance above and beyond the calls of duty would not put too fine a point on it as they far-excelled the mayhem of the normal 'thrash'. His knock-out golf tournaments, so aptly called, played from end to end of the Ante-room were a joy to behold, and a 'must' to participate, as spectators trapped behind settees or armchairs in the fairway were likely to be decapitated or knocked unconscious by the hook or slice of a slightly sloshed golfer, who would, in the event excuse the stroke on bad light, gale force winds or flatulence.

Other games played were variations on the standard gentle themes of RAF Mess parties resembling, and at times exceeding, the bloodiest battles for survival in the Roman arenas on a good day, and I think even Spartacus would have demanded double time or a kamikaze bonus.

Surprisingly, all these games were conducted in a most gentlemanly and courteous manner, a most refined hooliganism where good friends, temporarily opponents, would battle to the death with no quarter asked or given, and get up when the smoke cleared away, dishevelled and completely knackered and, ringing the bell for Rutherford, our stalwart Mess Steward, who would observe the action with a dispassionate yet benign look that belied his apparent disapproval of his young gentlemen playing silly buggers, would toast each other's health with great good humour.

One evening, during a lull in the proceedings, 'Batchy' commissioned a rather plastered intelligence officer named Gibson, who had been a commercial artist in Civvy Street, to draw larger-than-life figures of voluptuous ladies in diaphanous and near-diaphanous veils and drapes on the wall panels of the Ante-room. These were magnificent and quite inoffensive drawings in charcoal with even the hair-styles done in most meticulous and up to date fashions. Gibson candidly admitted that his artistic ability peaked in the late evening after a few snifters and he must have been blotto that night as the results were perfection.

At breakfast the following morning the Mess staff were just finishing the clearing of the debris of the night before, including the erasure of Gibson's masterpieces from the walls, when the Station Commander, Wing Commander Guy Carter, walked in. Guy Carter, a most charming man, who, sadly, did not survive the War, had flown in 41 Squadron in the 1914/18 War and, at the outbreak of War in September, had quickly majored on our Spitfires in an enthusiastic attempt to get into the action and sometimes, after a 'scramble' a lone Spitfire could be seen way behind us. It was Guy, chasing after the youthfulness that had been taken from him over 20 years before when he had taken part in the vicious dog-fights above the French battlefields.

He had been at the party and was livid that the works of

art were being erased and promptly organised another party so that Gibson could give a repeat performance.

'Batchy' was a brilliant pilot and could do things with an aeroplane that held one enthralled, not daring to emulate such mastery and artistry. One day one of our new Sergeant Pilots, in a Spitfire saw a Blenheim close to him and proceeded to carry out a practice astern attack but, before he could close and line up the Blenheim in his sights, it disappeared in a flick-roll. This manoeuvre, which throws excessive strain on an aircraft not suitably stressed can induce structural failure and is virtually impossible for a Blenheim type aircraft, but it was 'Batchy', and he finished up on the tail of the Spitfire. It shook the young pilot rigid and he had great difficulty in breaking away and then only by use of the excessive power and speed of the Spitfire, by which time it would have been much too late.

'Batchy' and I struck up a great friendship and I came to know him very well, listening for hours as he modestly explained how he did this or that and I prayed that some of his expertise and mastery of an aeroplane would rub off on me.

I remember so well his friendship that brooked no bounds of rank and position as, later in the War, I received a telephone call from him when he had become a very senior officer, inviting me to dine with him.

When I arrived and entered the Ante-room 'Batchy' was talking to a number of very senior Navy, Army and RAF officers with rank-braid up to their elbows. He broke away, greeted me warmly, and led me by the arm back to the circle of senior officers. "I'd like you all to meet Wally," he said, matter of factly, "He's a clever little chap and a great friend of mine" and introduced me to everyone present.

I enjoyed the evening immensely being put pleasantly at ease in such exalted company, but acutely conscious of my two and a half rings of a Squadron Leader, which looked thinner, by comparison with those around me, than the thin pilot-officer's stripe I had started with originally. I must admit that my ego soared beyond reason when I caught the quizzical glances of several distinguished officers who were pleased to accept me into their company, but, on leaving, common-sense returned, and deflated me as I acknowledged to myself that, despite my ambitions, I was most unlikely to reach promotion to the upper echelons of Service life.

* * *

The other 'character' to join the Station arrived suddenly by air one morning accompanied by the Group Air Officer Commanding's aid de camp (the personal assistant to the AOC). He was in total disgrace, only avoiding a court-martial and probable death by firing squad through the rapid air evacuation by the ADC.

His name was 'Wimpy' a white Staffordshire bull terrier of unprepossessing appearance, with the tip of one ear missing, but having unbounded energy and joie de vivre. Apparently the AOC's gold-braided headgear, the gold braid commonly called 'scrambled egg', had been dislodged from its special peg in the hall of the Mess at Group HQ and lay on the carpet unnoticed.

Wimpy, strolling past, and for some reason known only to himself, couldn't resist the temptation and relieved himself well and truly into the headgear and all over the scrambled egg. All hell broke loose and Wimpy was very lucky to escape with his life by the quick-thinking of the ADC.

All servicemen, strangely, are renowned for collecting pets and mascots, be they dogs, cats, parrots, geese, ducks and even nubile young damsels. Wimpy was, of course, gladly accepted into the Squadron and was observed the following day, after a battle for leadership, leading the parade of Station dogs who daily visited for tit-bits at the kitchens of the Officers, NCOs and Airmen's Messes.

The ground crew would get a large piece of cleaning rag and entice Wimpy to battle for it and when his jaws were firmly clamped on it would swing him round in a circle until shoulder high, the dog growling like mad but wise enough not to let go until lowered to the ground. One day a new airman swinging Wimpy round let go and poor Wimpy went a hell of a purler on the ground. Another airman clouted the offender and Wimpy got up, walked over and calmly bit him in the leg for ungentlemanly behaviour.

When the winter came the airmen made a slide on the frozen snow and ice and Wimpy thought it was a grand idea to chase after the men down the slide until the inevitable pile-up when Wimpy would finally emerge from underneath a heap of men with the wind knocked out of him but completely unruffled and ready for more. In the snow he was almost invisible but if one looked for two small red spheres Wimpy was not far away.

Much later, and just before we moved south to Hornchurch for the Dunkirk evacuation, Wimpy disgraced himself once more by going across the airfield to a farm to have fun chasing sheep. He had done no damage but the farmer demanded rightly that he be shot, a fate we would not let Wimpy suffer. A fragile compromise was reached when the farmer, knowing somehow that we were moving, offered to take him and try to teach him to become a sheep dog.

Knowing Wimpy, and fearing the worst, we sadly and very reluctantly parted with him never expecting to see him again. The airmen, bless them, were very upset and heaped going-away presents of bones and biscuits on Wimp.

Later, when the Squadron returned to Catterick on rest, we went over to the farm in some trepidation, fearing the worst. How surprised and pleased we were to see Wimpy, alive and very well indeed, slimmed down, still as tough as old rope but a completely changed man.

He walked out to us at the heel of the farmer, proudly, with a new dignity and air of responsibility, and only broke to greet us when the farmer spoke to him. Wimpy was overjoyed to see us again and then after effusive greetings walked calmly back to his new friend and master.

In 1943 I landed at Catterick to refuel and collect a lot of my kit which had remained there since the War began and found time to go over to see the farmer and Wimpy.

I was saddened to hear that the old dog had died a year before, but his epitaph, spoken by the farmer was most fitting for old Wimp.

"He was a bugger, with a mind of his own. He knew he was no bloody sheep-dog, but he tried, by God, he tried and he was a good friend, I miss the old chap." That was good enough for me and we had a whisky to drink old Wimpy down.

WIMPY. Ace mascot of The Foiting Foity Foist Single Seat Pursuit Squadron, Catterick 1939. With apologies to Errol Flynn and John Wayne.

In October 1939 we were suddenly warned of imminent squadron movement and, given a little time to pack small suitcases, which would travel with the ground crews and surplus pilots by transport aircraft, were ready to go. Our 12 Spitfires took off and, in excellent formation headed north for Scotland landing at Drem, east of Edinburgh to refuel. Without delay we headed north again, over the Firth of Forth and up over the grandeur of the Grampian mountains, crossing Moray Firth, into the Highlands until, just before reaching John O'Groats, we went into landing pattern and dropped down, on to the bleak and windy airfield at Wick.

Apparently the Luftwaffe had been carrying out considerable reconnaissance in the area and it was considered that there might be a threat to the naval base at Scapa Flow. We were to patrol way out to sea to intercept any intruders. As it turned out, in the short while we were there, we never saw anything except seagulls and Scottish trawlers as the Germans turned back long before we could get to them, but no doubt our patrols were effective.

Although I flew hundreds of hours in Spitfires at very low level over the Channel and its approaches later in the war, searching for ditched aircraft and crews, I can never forget the apprehension of those days of flying out over lonely cold northern waters for many miles when the chances of rescue, if one went down through engine failure, were absolutely nil. The slightest engine vibration or fancied variation of engine revolutions, pressure or temperature gauges, which was totally hallucinatory, gave one near heart failure.

The relief of crossing back over the coast was beyond

description, yet the Fleet Air Arm boys, with single engined Skuas and Rocs would scuttle about always over the water, up to Norway and heaven knows where else, miles from home, with indecent composure. For me, they were welcome to it but they had my heart-felt admiration.

We had been warned that Wick was 'dry' and urged to take a little liquid sustenance with us, but the luggage compartment of a Spitfire was a laughable tiny container in the fuselage, large enough to hold an overnight shaving kit and toothbrush and little else. We had stuffed the shaving kits in our tunic pockets and we each stowed a bottle of Scotch.

The Station or Railway Hotel provided quarters for all the pilots, and the NCOs and ground-crews were comfortably billeted in the town. To our great surprise and pleasure, Wick was far from being as 'dry' as forecast and we had an excellent time having a drink with the local people, who were great company.

When it was decided that our services were no longer required we returned to Catterick, calling in at Drem again to refuel. The bottles of Scotch were still 'virgo intacta', having been completely forgotten, so, during the refuelling, we trooped over to the dispersal where a very friendly Spitfire squadron were holding the fort and welcomed us bearing gifts, namely 12 bottles of good Scotch which were promptly broached and circulated.

To say the subsequent take-off and formation flying southwards was erratic would, indeed, again, be putting too fine a point on it. We did, however, manage to stay within sight of each other all the way, bobbing up and down like puppets, to land back at Catterick in what can best be described as an uncontrolled arrival.

Maintaining day and night readiness, interspersed with fruitless 'scrambles' the squadron was kept busy training replacement pilots arriving to make up the strength following the posting of several experienced pilots to newly-formed squadrons.

One of these 'new' boys, that is, new to us, being a pre-war regular officer with plenty of savoir-faire, was Pilot Officer Bill Stapleton. He was a big, charming, handsome fellow with a great sense of humour and an eye for the ladies, who slotted easily into the squadron and we were pleased to have him posted to us. He was very unlucky to be shot down by German ground fire on 1st June 1940 during one of our many patrols over the Dunkirk evacuation, to spend five miserable years as a POW.

Meeting him again for the first time after almost exactly 48 years he recalled his first familiarisation and formation exercise with Norman Ryder, shortly after his arrival at Catterick.

They took off normally, in open formation, and when airborne the impassive Norman beckoned to Bill to bring his Spitfire in closer, which he did. Norman then beckoned for Bill to come closer still, which he also did. To Bill's consternation the imperious and impatient finger of his leader beckoned again and again until the horrified Bill was almost in Norman's lap, the Spitfires literally inches apart, when, to Bill's massive relief, Norman appeared to be satisfied and put up his thumb to signal his approval.

Bill was committed, the point of no return, locked in very tight formation, sweating it out, clinging to Norman like a leech with the perspiration pouring from him, gently juggling his controls and throttle to keep his wing-tip in Norman's ear and his airscrew almost chewing the wing-tip of the other Spitfire, while Norman calmly and unconcernedly carried on with the exercise. It's something that eventually, and with a hell of a lot of practice, becomes acceptable and commonplace, but I knew the feeling.

In early November, during night-flying exercises, we were to suffer the loss of one of the old regulars of the squadron. Flying Officer 'Pooky' Overall, a most likeable and diminutive Canadian from Niagara Falls who crashed and was killed shortly after take-off. He had taken off normally but, when airborne veered to the right and, quite unaccountably, dived steeply into the village of Catterick.

'Pooky' was an excellent pilot and it was unlikely that he had omitted to check the tightness of the friction nut on his throttle quadrant, which prevents the throttle from sliding back unnoticed to the closed position, or had pulled up the aircraft too steeply in climb-out to cause it to stall. It was eventually considered that the engine of his Spitfire had started to syphon glycol coolant from the header tank producing dense clouds of white vapour which, entering his cockpit before he had time to close the canopy, may have disorientated him and possibly obscured his blind-flying panel.

The Spitfire crashed into a house. The occupants, a lady and her two children were fortunate to escape injury, but the mother, in writing to 'Pooky's' mother in sympathy, expressed some concern for the safety of her children in war-time England. Mrs Overall invited the children to stay with her in Niagara Falls for the duration of the war. The

Canadian Government were most considerate to pay their fares, a touching end that in death 'Pooky' should give safety and life to two young children.

Winter suddenly arrived and the airfield was blanketed in snow. Snow ploughs were produced and, with everyone on the Station shovelling frenziedly, it was possible to clear a single short, narrow, snow-packed runway for us to operate from. The snow was piled high each side of the runway with intersections at intervals for aircraft to gain access, with a narrow perimeter track alongside running down to the dispersals.

It was a very dodgy operation, taking off and landing in such conditions, particularly with the Spitfires having such restricted visibility when taxying, ploughing about in clouds of snow, pilots not knowing whether they were on or off the runway. In fact 'Buck' Ryan taxied out one day on a 'scramble' in a cloud of snow, missed the intersection and had actually opened his throttle to half power for take-off before he realised that he was not on the runway but still on the perimeter track. A few unsuspecting airmen walking down the perimeter track were horrified to see a Spitfire, tearing towards them, at full gallop. They dived head-first into the snow banks which melted rapidly from their invective.

Landing on packed snow in bright sunlight could be very tricky as, like landing an amphibian on still, glassy water, one's judgement of height could be so affected that one might hold off much too high or virtually fly into the deck with a resounding thump. One of 'Batchy's' pearls of wisdom was, "Get the feel in these, lad" extending his beautifully long and sensitive fingers and rubbing the tips together. "Failing which," he added with a broad smile, "Use the seat of your trousers, the best judge of height in the business". By God, he was right; it worked, believe me.

We became accustomed to our restricted existence in the flimsy wooden dispersal huts, continuing with more ineffective scrambles, convoy patrols and training exercises for the time that must inevitably arrive when we should be committed to battle and put to the test.

Most of us at this time had been in the Squadron a long while and were all firm friends, aware of each other's ability, limitations and strength of purpose. We were united and confined in the small world of a fighter squadron at war and, sitting in the crew-room at readiness, for hours at a time, had many guarded conversations, kept deliberately in off-hand vein, on our attitudes to forthcoming battles. Strangely, and without definite admission, these were almost identical. The dreams and ambitions originating in early boyhood had now developed to an acceptance of whatever fate had in store.

We had all been given the opportunity we had sought so eagerly, to become fighter pilots. We had trained very hard and, although lacking battle experience, knew that in due time we must justify our existence. Our common fear, though undeclared and typically British, of not 'putting up a good show', not letting the side down (and the squadron in particular) 'and not making a bloody fool of oneself', was paramount.

We silently considered the thought of violent death, without comment, but had an admitted dread of severe and crippling injury and survival, most particularly the horror of terrible disfigurement from burns.

It never occurred to us that we should know the gnawing apprehensions of the question at the end of each day. "Is it to be my turn next tomorrow, or the day after, or when?" The fear of anticipation, the torturing thought must be put firmly aside and, for good or ill, fate left to decide one's harsh uncertainty of existence. Statistics have shown that the expectation of life for pilots in combat in the 1914/1918 War was eight weeks, but I was unaware that in 1940 this time was to be reduced to 84 hours.

War brings out the very best and, sadly, the very worst in man and there were, in most squadrons, types who, so obviously, saw the occasion as an opportunity for self-aggrandisement, rapid promotion and the collection of decorations. These, 'Errol Flynns' displayed a feckless bravado, often construed as heroic fearlessness, which made them a danger to themselves and also unfortunately, to those closely involved. A man in battle, with a drained hollow feeling in the pit of his stomach, the sand-dry throat, nerves stretched almost to breaking point, fights no less staunchly, but with dogged determination and the hope of self-preservation, the thin life-line to survival.

The distance from Catterick to the coast wasted valuable time and aircraft flying hours and, in February 1940, the small grass airfield at West Hartlepool (Greatham) was taken over as a forward base from which we operated four aircraft from dawn to dusk on 'scrambles', convoy and coastal patrols. Our ground crews, being capable of providing important and even secret information, direct from the horse's mouth, let me in on the secret of the mushroom field next to the airfield perimeter, which could be reached by worming one's way through rolls of defensive barbed wire.

Later, (in June) and being over-partial to mushrooms, I was soon in on the act, wriggling through the wire despite torn uniform and lacerations and gouges on face, hands, knees, back and backside. One morning at dawn, while the other pilots snoozed in the crew-room, I had collected the most wonderful hatful of mushrooms when the scramble bell sounded. Being the wrong side of the wire, I tried in my haste, as my fitter started up my Spitfire to save time, to dive headlong through the hole we had made and came out the other side bloodied but unbowed, sans tunic, sans trousers and, worst of all, sans bloody mushrooms. I didn't mind about wrecking my uniform but, oh, those lovely wasted lost mushrooms.

Taking the early session from dawn we would be relieved between 9 am and 10 am and return to Catterick for breakfast and bath and a shave. On arrival at base my aircraft was often easily recognisable, the Spitfire waltzing around in the circuit, bobbing hither and thither as I sat balancing a hatful of precious mushrooms on my knees while doing all the necessary things in the 'office', changing hands on the control column to select under-carriage down, changing back for flaps down, canopy open, and the necessary throttle work to get down without bruising or losing my breakfast.

'Scrambled' one day from West Hartlepool for a 'bogey' at 15,000 feet I took off with two rather new Sergeant pilots and under a heavy cloud base of 500 feet headed out to sea on a south easterly 'vector' from Control. We climbed up into cloud, the sergeant pilots holding good, tight formation on either side of me and, after nearly fifteen minutes we were still in the 'heavy stuff' with the formating aircraft becoming a little ragged under the strain and beginning to 'hunt', which was a bad sign. Control came on transmission, weakly in the static and said the 'bogey' had gone home, and so could we.

We were still climbing in cloud and I was almost prepared to give a breakaway order as the two Spitfires were getting dangerous when, to our great relief we broke top cloud at 20,000 feet into brilliant sunshine. I estimated our position as best I could and, setting a reciprocal course, settled the formation down. I had been reluctant to give a breakaway in cloud on the climb as the two pilots would have had great difficulty in changing over to independent blind flying on instruments and I thought it was expecting too much of them to put them through a protracted formation descent.

Briefing them quickly, I gave instructions to break away and let down through the cloud individually to sea level, fly in to the coast and return to Catterick around the Cleveland Hills, if weather permitted or land back at West Hartlepool.

Knowing where I was – famous last words – and some minutes after the two Spitfires had gone, I let down into the murk and, when down to 400 feet had not broken cloud base. A moment later I looked out, to see, not water, but dry, very dry land and I was now only at 300 feet.

Ampleforth College went whistling past at eye-level and I realised with a shock what had happened. I had completely misjudged my rate of descent and, instead of breaking cloud base out over the sea, I had, by some miracle, headed inland, still in cloud, at the only possible place without hitting the hills. The low, narrow gap between Filey and Scarborough extended westwards, south of Pickering and Helmsley, over Oswaldkirk, past the College and on to the York-Darlington railway line below Thirsk.

I turned right, almost brushing the tree-tops under the low cloud and headed up the Great North Road to Catterick feeling very chastened, realising how foolish and over-confident I had been, nearly writing off a perfectly good Spitfire, and myself, in the process. I had wasted one of my nine, but felt it was well worth it, admitting to myself that I still had a hell of a lot to learn.

On 3 April 1940, the RAF and 41 Squadron, lost it's first Spitfire to the Luftwaffe, the first British fighter to be shot down protecting the shores of England during the War.

Group Captain Norman Ryder, CBE, DFC and Bar, then a Flight Lieutenant in our squadron took off from West Hartlepool in atrocious weather conditions to intercept a Heinkel 111 bomber reported attacking coastal shipping.

He attacked the bomber, forcing it to ditch in the rough sea, but was unfortunate to receive return fire which forced him to ditch also, the first time a Spitfire was to go 'in the drink'. One of the fishing trawlers in the vicinity rescued the German crew and another saved Norman, but only after he had gone down with the Spitfire to a considerable depth before being able to free himself and rise to the surface. His very detailed report on the ditching provided invaluable information for Spitfire squadrons.

Norman was in 41 when I joined it long before the War, a man of great intelligence, talent, ability and humour and I treasure his friendship. He fought with distinction, from the outset of war, through Dunkirk, the Battle of Britain and the offensive sweeps over France, eventually being shot down in 1942 being taken prisoner and joining Bill Stapleton in the 'Bag'.

* * *

The days of the 'Phoney War' ended when the German blitzkrieg swept across Europe and the Netherlands, and Belgium collapsed to the onslaught. The French armies, that had not quickly surrendered (like many, putting up only token resistance) retreated across France with the British Expeditionary Force to the Channel coast concentrating on a massive evacuation from around the port of Dunkirk, back to England. The Hurricane squadrons based in France performed epic feats as they fought desperately against the overwhelming odds of the Luftwaffe fighters and it was obvious that we should be committed before long.

Despite violent pressures, our Fighter Command leader, the brilliant, Air Chief Marshall 'Stuffy' Dowding had successfully blocked attempts to despatch Spitfire Squadrons to operate in France to bolster the collapsing situation. He knew that the German steam-roller could not be halted by such action, and it would have lost him the iron fist he needed to repel the invasion and subjugation of England he had long foreseen as Hitler's vengeful and ultimate aim.

One of the arguments in defence of his adamant policy was that Spitfires, being less rugged than Hurricanes and with narrow undercarriages, could not have operated successfully out of small emergency fields in France without incurring excessive non-combat losses of aircraft on the ground. We understood and applauded his decision but were a little hurt at the slight reflection on our abilities when we knew we could have flown in to and out of a French chicken-run, blindfolded and half-cut, given a couple of yards extra run.

In May 1940, as the Allies retreated in disarray before the German onslaught, the BEF, deserted and unsupported on their flanks, fighting with supreme gallantry retreated to the small bridgehead at Dunkirk in an attempt to evacuate nearly 500,000 men from the docks and beaches. What followed is a glorious chapter in British history as the Royal Navy, supported by hundreds of small boats, manned by volunteer sailors, performed a miracle in rescuing most of that gallant band of men.

We were despatched south to Hornchurch to relieve the Spitfires of 54 Squadron which had been involved in heavy fighting in covering patrols over the beaches and inland from Dunkirk, intercepting the German bombers and fighters attacking the bridgehead.

Briefed to take-off in the pre-dawn darkness about 3 am the squadron climbed out in tight formation, in radio silence, up through the low cloud and, at reduced speed to conserve fuel. We headed for the French coast to arrive at the first light of dawn over Dunkirk, where a thick, black column of smoke from burning oil tanks and vehicles rose to a great height.

We could operate over the area on patrol for at least one hour, making allowance for rapid fuel consumption in any skirmish, with just sufficient left in the tanks to return at low level across the channel to refuel at Manston, by Ramsgate.

Prior to their departure for a well earned rest to Catterick the previous evening the CO and pilots of 54 Squadron, 'Prof.' Leathart, Al Deere, Colin Gray, George Gribble and John Allan (who had joined the RAF with me), who had distinguished themselves from the outset and were to excel themselves later in the Battle of Britain, had given us the benefit of their experience and, with subdued and mixed feelings, we droned on towards France.

I well recall my own feelings, mostly relief that at last the waiting was over and the testing time was here. We had all, with varying degree of application, mastered our trade and the devil was waiting to take the hindmost. Looking across the silent formation, the Spitfires rising and falling imperceptably, I could see the hunched figures of my friends, the masked faces giving no indication of the thoughts within.

They were all so close that it was almost possible to reach out and touch each one, yet we were completely detached, a million miles apart, self-contained and quite alone in a tiny cockpit, where no-one could give any assistance to another if hit or injured, but only watch helplessly and wait for it to end. At least the 'bomber boy' crews could talk to each other on the inter-com. to bolster a flagging spirit, but the cockpit of the fighter is at times a lonely place. Yet one felt an invisible life-line which gave some consolation.

Our patrols to intercept the German bombers and fighters took us well inland from the French coast and we had some difficulty in maintaining contact with our Control at Dover.

We had to relinquish our new and more powerful VHF radio sets and re-install our old HF sets, in case the Germans obtained one of the more advanced sets from a crashed aircraft. The older sets were much less efficient. The Germans could, very craftily, come up on our frequency and give misleading instructions in perfect English in the middle of a patrol which our Control could not receive and contradict. We fell easily for a 'Pancake' (return to base) instruction once before our patrol time was up. But, on the second occasion, we acknowledged the order and moved away down the coast screeching "Pancake, Pancake", belting back flat out some minutes later when the Luftwaffe, believing the target was unpatrolled before a relief squadron could arrive, had moved in to bomb and strafe.

Our strategy was most successful, the Germans getting a lot more than they had bargained for. 'Lulu' Lovell, having run out of ammunition, chased and harassed a Junkers 88 bomber so closely, at very low level, that, in taking violent evasive action, the 88 touched a wing on the beach, cartwheeled and blew up. I was close on Lulu's tail with ammo left to back him up, but one must admit that to have a deadly Spitfire right up one's bum at 50 yards, ammo or no ammo had to be a shattering experience.

Lulu was to repeat this hairy trick later on in a battle over Kent. Out of ammo he dropped down over the Coast to sea level and caught up with a couple of ME 109s returning hurriedly to their French base. Halfway across the Channel they were joined in loose formation astern by, as they thought, one of their own friends, not in the least expecting a mad Irishman for company. Lulu's description of the subsequent action was hilarious. "We were going along nicely when suddenly there was a scream of 'Achtung,

Schpitfeuer' and the 109s split-arsed away in complete shock, one heading left for Norway and the other turning right for Spain, most unsociably. Can I claim for the two probables, full of twitch and out of petrol?" He couldn't, but deserved full marks for a bit of applied psychology.

One other incident which served to brighten the day occurred early one morning as the squadron lifted off from Hornchurch in formation climbing up into low cloud. A sergeant pilot, who must remain anonymous was flying No. 3 to me in a section on the starboard side of the formation as we went into the cloud.

He was erratic, not holding a tight position and gradually waffled so much that he lost me completely, disappearing in the murk. We broke top cloud some minutes later and, keeping radio silence, I looked around for my No. 3, somewhere I hoped to my right. He wasn't there, but lo and behold – way off to my left on the other side of the squadron was my wandering boy.

Instead of keeping a heading on his own on the starboard side until he had broken cloud, and then rejoining his station, he had felt a little lonely and edged his way to his left looking for company, somehow flying right through the squadron in cloud without hitting anyone. It's all part of life's rich pattern, but at the crack of dawn, with a bit of a hangover, one can do without these little sideshows, they're inclined to give one the early morning twitch.

During our patrols we were often 'pooped at' by Flak sent up indiscriminately by gunners of all nationalities, who obviously hated aeroplanes and shot happily at friend and foe alike. One pilot, on his first patrol over Dunkirk, came up on the R/T unbelievably, enquiring, "What are all those black puffs?"

Resisting the overwhelming temptation to reply, "Them's Negro homosexuals, sonny," one had to drop back on the hackneyed reply "That's Flak, you bloody fool" and explained, "If you can see it and hear it you're reasonably safe, but if you see it about two feet from your aircraft you won't hear it – you'll be dead. If it gets really thick and your engine stops, you can get out and walk on it. Now stop asking silly bloody questions and get back into formation!"

Until the Dunkirk evacuation was finally completed a fortnight later the Squadron carried out several patrols each day, sometimes in foul weather, from first light until darkness and gained considerable combat experience. It is known that the Navy and Army forces at Dunkirk bitterly accused the RAF of not giving support and low cover to the evacuation but many of them on the spot failed to understand that such cover of fighters, swanning at low level above the beaches for reassurance, would be totally ineffective.

With limited resources and the distance involved the patrols had to make use of every moment, sweeping inland to intercept, disrupt and bring down the Luftwaffe before they could get into attacking positions. In any case Dunkirk was a very unhealthy place to fly over, the Navy and Army rightly regarding anything in the air as hostile, putting up all the anti-aircraft fire they could muster.

On the 1 June, my old chum, Bill Stapleton went missing after an early morning patrol. There had been a mêlée during which we had become separated and, calling him on the R/T, low on petrol, I headed for Manston, telling him to get out and home. However, on his way out, after trying to 'duff' a German airfield on his own, he was hit by ground fire and went into the 'drink' just a couple of hundred yards out to sea. He was pulled out, injured, by the Germans and, sadly, went into a POW camp until the end of the War.

He was, and still is, bless him, a grand character, an excellent pilot, full of the joys of Spring and good humour. Commissioned in the RAF at 18 before the War he joined 41 Squadron in 1939 and, returning home in 1945, picked up the threads of his shattered career to retire as a Wing Commander in 1964, being awarded the CBE for his services.

* * *

In late June our squadron returned to Catterick to rest, after having been involved in heavy fighting, with some losses, but acquitting themselves well in the squadron's 'blooding', with experience gained to stand them in good stead later.

Before leaving Hornchurch an incident had occurred that had the Station rocking with laughter. A new sergeant pilot, taking off in a Spitfire, committed a cardinal error. He failed to check the incipient swing of the aircraft, due to the torque, which, if not corrected immediately, can lead to an embarrassing and dangerous situation. As he opened the throttle wider the swing became more uncontrollable and, instead of throttling back and aborting the take-off, careered across the airfield. Too late, he awoke to the fact that he was travelling at right angles to his intended take-off path, and was heading for one of the hangars when he decided to pull back his throttle.

The Spitfire, luckily slowing down, rammed the front

wall of the hangar and entered a large office where a senior Warrant Officer in charge of aircraft maintenance was seated, busy at his desk. The wing of the Spitfire went past his head and the airscrew and nose embedded themselves in the rear wall at it came to a halt.

In a cloud of dust and plaster the Warrant Officer, one of the old school and seemingly unperturbed by the intrusion, rose from his desk, climbed through wreckage on to the wing of the Spitfire and bounced his fist on the head of the dazed but uninjured sergeant pilot in the cockpit. He said "That's to remind you to observe my seniority. The next time you come into my bloody office, knock the bloody door" accentuating each word with another thump, and as imperturbably stepped down, brushed one of the thousand specks of dust from his uniform and walked away.

* * *

For a while after arriving back at Catterick we felt ill at ease. So much had recently happened, and yet the Station we knew so well hadn't changed at all and, perhaps, we had been dreaming, but faces were missing and we were not the same young pilots that had flown away a few short weeks before. The pilots of 54 Squadron had rested well and were ready to return to Hornchurch leaving us to our own devices.

The tension eased and once more we practised to make use of the hard lessons we had learned. Each pilot was given a few days leave, although the squadron was held at readiness.

The Germans, now virtual Masters of Europe, were

regrouping, to bring the bomber and fighter squadrons close up to the French and Belgian Coasts. It was obvious that the attack on Britain would not be long delayed and, if the Luftwaffe gained superiority in the air, invasion of England would quickly follow.

Production of aircraft, particularly the Hurricanes lost in France and Spitfires over Dunkirk, had to be increased and, under Lord Beaverbrook as Chief of the Ministry of Aircraft production, miracles were performed. The training of pilots was a slow process, although new squadrons were being formed to bolster the strength of Fighter Command. The total of fully trained and experienced fighter squadrons was pitifully small compared with the prodigious array of German bombers and fighters, manned mostly by battle-hardened veterans being prepared for their assault on Britian. The die was cast.

* * *

With little pause after Dunkirk the Luftwaffe began to mount their air offensive and the southern sectors of 11 and 10 Groups bore the brunt of attacks, the Battle of Britain being deemed to have started in earnest on the 10 July. The pilots of 54 Squadron at Hornchurch had been heavily engaged since 1 July and, though sadly depleted, had been giving a noble account of themselves. They, and other squadrons in 11 Group, had reached a point of near exhaustion and badly needed rest and re-equipment when in mid July we were despatched south once more to relieve them.

There were successive phases of the ensuing battle, starting with the Luftwaffe probing the defences, heavily attacking coastal shipping convoys bringing badly needed supplies of food, fuel and equipment from America to our beleagured country. The harbour and oil installations were subjected to dive-bombing and high level attacks, followed by attempts to obliterate our forward airfields which were badly damaged but somehow remained operational. The radar control stations came under fire and the Germans extended their bomber raids to airfields close to London, and eventually to London itself.

In the brief space of time since Dunkirk we, the 'old hands' still with the squadron, who had been together for quite a while since pre-war days, had very similar thoughts on what was before us. Flying down once more to Hornchurch, I am sure that we all had one thought uppermost, that 41 Squadron of proud motto – 'SEEK AND DESTROY', would stand and be counted. We were aware that the air fighting would be over the Channel and southern England, which gave us a faint sense of assurance that, although in a defensive role, we stood some little chance of survival, but we were not prepared for what was to follow.

After landing, and while our aircraft were being refuelled, we chatted to the pilots of 54 Squadron who gave us the latest 'Gen', and wished us luck before taking off for Catterick to 'rest'.

The atmosphere at Hornchurch had, of necessity, changed completely and there was now a powerful, but subdued, sense of urgency in the air. The Luftwaffe bombers were attacking the large merchant shipping convoys all along the South Coast up the Channel to Dover and the Thames Estuary, while JU 87 dive-bombers made repeated assaults on Dover Harbour.

The squadron was quickly committed to constant scrambles and patrols in strength covering the convoys and, with other squadrons, moved down to Manston, near Ramsgate. The Jerries soon became aware of this, bombing the airfield and forcing our withdrawal to Hornchurch. Subsequently we would fly down to Manston at first light, disperse as best we could, returning to Hornchurch at dusk.

The ME 109s were very active, free-chasing and 'jumping' Spitfires and Hurricanes on convoy patrol cover and we were involved in many skirmishes from high to low level over the Channel.

Although still generally flying in 'Vics' of three aircraft we had now modified our intercept lay-out to a wider line-abreast formation, when 'trade' was about, and which later became the 'finger four' principle. In addition, and despite the 'Dowding Spread' policy of gun harmonisation at 300 yards, our 8 Brownings were reduced to a cone of fire of 150 yards that we could press home each attack to maximum effect.

At Manston, when at readiness, there was generally a poker school in progress and the betting was often quite heavy. On the principal that one couldn't get out to spend it and couldn't take it with one it was commonplace to see the most reckless bets and bluffs being made.

One day Douglas Gamblen, one of the 'old' boys, who normally did not bet heavily, was piling in the cash holding a good hand when we were 'scrambled'. The cards were always left on the table face down with the 'pot' so that the players could continue on their return, but it was a rule that if a player was more than 10 minutes late after the others had landed to refuel he would relinquish his stake and be eliminated in that hand.

Douglas knew he was on to a winning hand but was delayed by some 109s who, spitefully, didn't want him to win the jackpot and kept him chatting. As the players were reseated and just about to declare Douglas out of the hand a Spitfire came rocketing in to a fast landing and taxied like mad to the dispersal. Within yards the engine stopped, the side flap dropped and as the Spitfire slowed to a walking pace a small figure baled out and ran like mad towards the poker game.

"If you rotters have pinched my money I'll 'do' the bloody lot of you," said a very breathless Douglas, "I make it 9 minutes and 50 seconds," and sat down, picked up his cards and scooped the pool, quite oblivious to the holes in his Spitfire which were not there at take off.

The ME 109s were adept at decoy, with top cover to 'jump' any interception and, early one morning the 29 July, which I shall always remember, Douglas and I were caught in this manner.

We dived steeply over Dover after a 109 and Douglas was in range to fire when I saw two 109s above and behind. I screamed at Douglas to break away but in his concentration to fire my desperate call went unheeded or unheard and, too late, one of the 109s poured concentrated fire into the Spitfire as he dived. Whether the other 109 fired at me I know not, but I was unscathed as I broke away violently, and turned back quickly to see Douglas's Spitfire, smoking badly, drop down to the Channel below, and I imagine he must have been killed at once by the burst of fire from his attacker. As the aircraft hit the water, broke up and disappeared I cursed the whole messy business of war and bidding Douglas, my old friend, farewell, turned sadly for base.

The same day, we were heavily engaged intercepting the JU 87 dive-bombers attacking shipping in Dover Harbour and, at the end of the day, had lost four Spitfires to the covering swarm of 109s, luckily without injury to all the pilots, Webster, Mackenzie, Scott and Bennions. With Lulu getting 'clobbered' and slightly injured the day before, we were now in the thick of it and fully committed.

After one of these attacks, 'Robin' Hood, our CO found himself in mid-Channel low over the water and, returning to base, met some JU 87s head-on returning to France, looking back over their shoulders for tail-chasing Spitfires and least expecting one in front. 'Robin', apart from putting the fear of God into the pilots, had some success in damaging several in this and several similar instances and probably caused several to go 'arse over tip' in attempting to land back in France in a state of shock.

During all this time we had not totally neglected the fun and frolic of high-spirited pilots in off-duty moments, but we were generally too tired and nerve-tensed at the end of a long day but to have a few drinks in the Mess and fall asleep in the process.

Often we headed for London to do a round of the pubs and clubs with an occasional theatre visit, but they were pale imitations of days gone by. The days of wine and roses had disappeared, along with old friends, and a more subdued form of winding down was the norm, although spirits would rise in inverse ratio to the spirits downed. On one occasion the girls of the Windmill Theatre were invited down to Hornchurch for a little party which lasted well into the following morning. George the Greek played haunting music on his guitar until, very sloshed, he fell off his stool and slept where he fell. The boys, with the hell of a hangover, flew with a new found zest after this 'thrash' and the girls deserved a medal for contributing so wholeheartedly to the war effort.

The Luftwaffe continued their massive attacks on shipping and harbour installations, using 109s to shoot down the harbour barrage balloons to clear the way for the bombers. Constantly they were probing to discover weaknesses in our defences but July, the first month of the Battle of Britain, ended without the Germans, despite the weight of attack, being able to exploit localised successes.

The weather in July had been indifferent and not conducive to really massive all-out daylight assaults by the Luftwaffe heavy bombers held on readiness and the first few days of August were relatively quiet as the Channel convoys were reduced to a fraction of the July figures. To Dowding and his Group Commanders this 'eye' of the hurricane of aggression could herald but one thing, preparation for the fulfilment of Hitler's rabid dream – the complete elimination of Britain as a power, and subjugation of its people.

Hermann Goering's air commanders were grouping their forces in prodigious numbers in the occupied territories, ready to swamp our defences and reduce our fighter squadrons to an impotent force before their day of reckoning – the invasion of Great Britain.

If, as has been recorded, Hitler had doubts of the success of the invasion with which he did not acquaint his commanders, believing that the subjugation of Russia was almost a pre-requisite, he could have obtained ample evidence that his doubts would be confirmed.

The British people, deeply stirred by the historic speeches of Winston Churchill, speeches that held no promise but warned of the dangers and hardships that must be faced with resolution and determination, were united, in no mood to bow their heads to the aggressor.

This wonderful attitude, this strength of purpose, transmitted to us, daily fighting never-ending battles, unaware, in our cloistered actions, of the responsibility being placed on our shoulders. It gave us a renewed determination to fight on regardless.

The first week of August passed with considerable activity and some success against free-chasing 109s in the Dover area, without loss to ourselves, and on the morning of the 8th three of us intercepted a large formation of 109s sighted near Manston looking for 'game'.

Diving from 25,000 feet to 12,000 feet I attacked one 109 with a short burst from close astern backed up by Terry and this aircraft went straight into the sea. In the mêlée that followed I managed to close right up behind another 109 firing a short burst which sent it diving steeply into the Channel.

As so often happens after a combat, the sky in the immediate vicinity emptied of aircraft, as if by magic, and I was alone. Returning to Manston I landed, and, seeing no squadron aircraft on the ground at dispersal, took off again at full bore, realising that the fight might still be in progress. Climbing to 12,000 feet again, I intercepted a lone 109 returning home and attacked, again with a very short burst from 50 yards, which caused this aircraft to crash into the sea.

Lulu, who had been having oxygen trouble, missed all this action but, although all my enemy aircraft were seen to crash, and Terry claimed three more 109s, we were not, in the final assessment by Intelligence, credited with the six aircraft we had shot down.

Momentarily, we were a little disheartened, after 'working over a hot stove' all morning, particularly as we were convinced that the close-quarter accuracy of our fire had to be totally effective and final, but what did it really matter, and who were we to argue? It was another case of the 'quick and the dead' and, by Christ, you had to be quick. The pre-requisite of status of a tally of 'kills' and a 'gong' or two were not in my book, only the necessity of doing what one could, as best one was able, hopefully walking away, until the next time.

The sight of a row of miniature swastikas on the fuselage of a Spitfire or Hurricane, denoting 'kills', did nothing for me, but the vision of my scalp on the side of a 109 pleased me even less. Neither did I 'go a bundle' on the practice of substituting personal initials on the fuselage instead of the normal squadron letters, with a painted pennant of a Squadron or Wing Leader to complete the picture.

This, in my humble opinion, was an invitation to the Jerries to single out and have a go at the top man, an invitation that needed no repetition. I suppose that this probably derived from the 1914/18 Air War, and that Von Richtofen, The Red Baron's Fokker tri-plane was painted all red, but then he was a German and probably hadn't been to an English Public School 'like wot we 'ad' and my contemporaries were being just a little 'de-trop', playing cowboys and indians.

I kept my thoughts to myself and just hoped that there would be some 'future' for us when it all ended.

* * *

In the afternoon of the 8th we were relieved by 54 Squadron again, 'homing' once more to Catterick to rest, and the same sense of unreality returned in the peaceful Yorkshire countryside, but it was grand to be home again.

On the 11 August I had the unusual experience of attacking a reconnaissance Junkers JU 88 bomber in cloud. It was intercepted at 17,000 feet over Thirsk and dived for cloud cover at 10,000 feet. I followed it into cloud closing to 25 yards to fire and was so close that I throttled back, in fear of ramming, for which the Spitfire was not designed. It was an eerie feeling as the flash of the eight guns lit up the cloud, when the port engine was hit by my first burst of fire. Another burst followed as we played a terrible game of cat and mouse in and out of the cloud. The crippled 88 eventually dropped down below cloud base where 'Mitzi' Darling, my number 2 was waiting to attack and it crashed near Whitby, three of its crew being taken prisoner.

Following the furious attacks by the Luftwaffe on Southern England on the 13th and 14th August, the Germans mounted a massive offensive on the 15th, which was considered by some to be the heaviest day's fighting of the entire Battle, extending from the South Coast up to the northern sectors.

While large forces of bombers and fighters attacked in the south the Luftwaffe massed a raid of over 100 Heinkel 111 and ME 110 aircraft from Denmark and Norway to attack targets in the Newcastle, Sunderland area, while another force of JU 88s attacked airfields in Yorkshire.

41 Squadron was airborne just before lunch and supported by other Spitfire Squadrons in the Durham area, made contact with the bombers, causing heavy losses and damage to 13 German aircraft without any loss to the squadron and, in the whole operation, the Luftwaffe suffered losses of over 20% of their aircraft involved.

Slightly bent Heinkel 111

Due to the continued effective resistance to raids against the south, the Germans were convinced that the northern sectors had been deprived of fighters to provide this defence, unaware that Dowding's policy of rotation of squadrons to and from the south 'on rest' still provided experienced battle-tested squadrons in the northern groups. Such simple flexibility could not be imagined and interpreted by the Germans in their Intelligence appreciation of Fighter Command, and they paid dearly for their mistake, the first, and last flank attack by daylight against the north ending in dismal, shattering failure.

Apart from fruitless scrambles after reconnaissance aircraft and convoy patrols the remainder of the month on rest passed reasonably quietly, 'Shippy', downing a Heinkel 111 off Flamborough Head to relieve the monotony.

Meanwhile the Battle raged in the south and we were impatient and fretful not to be taking part. The Luftwaffe attacks were intensified, targets including radar-stations, factories, harbour installations and all fighter airfields including those closer to London; Kenley, Biggin Hill, Croydon, Northolt and Hornchurch.

During one of Hermann Goering's tirades against his air commanders, for their failure to produce any lasting impression on Fighter Command, he brushed aside their claim that their ME 109s had been successful in the free-chasing role, and insisted that even closer close cover support should be given to the bomber formations, a shackling of experienced pilots that was to prove to be a most critical error.

The Junkers 87 Stuka bombers were withdrawn following crushing losses, and three times in four days the Luftwaffe lost more than 50 aircraft in a day. Goering gave almost complete free rein to his commanders in their choice of targets, the attacks widening to airfields, towns and targets of opportunity well inland, in poor weather conditions.

Towards the end of August we were once again brought to readiness for departure to Hornchurch, our second home, where 54 Squadron had, with many losses, (including Johnny Allen, who had joined the RAF with me) been continuously engaged until their pilots were again on the verge of total exhaustion. The Luftwaffe had paid dearly in the process. The Squadron, so ably led by 'Prof' Leathart with very experienced pilots like Al Deere, Colin Grey, George Gribble and Eric Edsall spear-heading their interceptions, had taken a magnificent toll of victories from the hordes of bombers and escorting fighters now swarming over Southern England. They fully deserved a respite.

* * *

We landed at Hornchurch to a different scene. The airfield had been bombed several times, destroying and damaging hangars and buildings, including the Operations Room, and causing many casualties. War had arrived on the doorstep of London, and on London itself when, on the 24 August, bombs were dropped on the south eastern quarter of the City, intended for the oil refineries of Thameshaven and Rochester, and the first to be dropped on London since 1918.

In the days that followed we were subjected to the shock of seeing very large numbers of bombers, Heinkel 111s, Junkers 88s and Dornier 17s, escorted closely by an equivalent number of ME 109 and ME 110 fighters, heading over the Coast and up the Thames Estuary. The sky was a mass of formations of German aircraft and it was incredible and unbelievable that this could be happening.

It struck us, even the most stout-hearted, like a douche of iced-cold water, to make one swallow hard and try to come to terms with the situation. It was a nasty dream, a nightmare, a totally unacceptable sight over our England.

As the squadron swung in to the attack, splitting to two flights of six Spitfires, one to attack and break up the leading formation of bombers and the other to stave off the escorting fighters, one realised that the moment of truth had finally arrived.

Instinctively, one looked around and behind for support, to relieve the responsibility for personal action, and there was nothing there, but a few old friends, doing and thinking exactly the same as yourself. Then, strangely, the inevitability of it all became apparent and one bowed to it.

Although we were, of course, quite unaware of it, the unremitting daylight air offensive was, for the first time, causing a lowering of morale in the Bomber and Fighter squadrons of the Luftwaffe. The bombers were paying a heavy daily toll in aircraft and crews, the ME 110 twin-engined fighters were no match for our Spitfires and Hurricanes and had their hands full defending themselves rather than defending the bombers. The ME 109 pilots were resentful of and frustrated by their implicit orders to stay close to the bombers, and dismayed at their mounting losses.

German Intelligence had wildly exaggerated their reports of British fighter losses as Fighter Command repeatedly penetrated the escorts, and there was a growing exhaustion in the Luftwaffe influenced by the heavy losses, the frustration and the hatred and fear of crossing the Channel, the 'Shite Kanal' and flying over enemy territory where capture or death were a high priority for the careless, or unfortunate.

Had they but realised it, they had the advantage of attack, in that they could choose the time and the place, to feint or punch hard, keeping our fighter squadrons in demoralising apprehension and nervous exhaustion.

Dowding was having to dig deeply into the reserves of men and machines, and the pilots had, of necessity, to find the stamina to last the long course. One evening, a most pertinent comment was made by a very wise senior officer, which gave us food for thought.

At dusk we had been released to the Mess, stood down for the night, and, having a few well-earned jars of ale, were joined by this officer. "Despite being a highly disorganised, insubordinate, drunken rabble," said he, for openers, with a smile, "I think you chaps deserve a drink with me, and do you know why?" We admitted we didn't know why, not wishing to point out that with his rank he could afford the round far better than we could, and, in any case, we were always ready at the drop of a hat, to drink with anyone who was willing to keep the lotion coming.

The drinks having arrived, and whiskys at that, we were in receptive mood and he began – "To say the situation will, before long, become 'touch and go' would not put too fine a point on it, but desperate occasions do require desperate remedies and, though you may think the limit is not far distant, you must know that this situation demands a total and unremitting certainty of purpose."

"Whatever happens, you *have* to maintain your effort, because you have the ability and you have, above all, the strength of purpose. Good night, chaps and good luck."

As he walked away I added, beneath my breath, as if to

complete his unfinished sentence, "And, by Christ, you'll bloody need it!", which, I thought afterwards, was very churlish of me and a bit uncalled for. He had, unconsciously, again reminded us of 41 Squadron's motto 'Seek and Destroy' and I like to think we benefited from his advice, and that his words gave us equal stimulation to the whiskys he had stood us.

Leaping Lena I

My rigger's artistry on the engine cowling is an impression of a Pterodactyl – like bird screwing the neck of Hitler's vulture.

On 5 September the day started well for the squadron, but was to end in a terrible shambles.

Mid morning we were airborne at full strength, 12 Spitfires intercepting a large formation of Dornier 17s with about 50 ME 109 escorts, at 16,000 feet and 22,000 feet, flank and rear cover, over Gravesend. We had the height advantage from 27,000 feet, worth a pot of gold, and went downstairs at a rate of knots.

'Robin' Hood, our CO was leading and, although rather 'rusty' in tactics, had the heart of a lion. The radio crackled as he detached 'A' Flight, under Norman Ryder, to give us cover against the 109s. I was petrified, but had to grin at the order, six Spitfires against so many 109s was a bloody tall order but the imperturbable Norman calmly acknowledged it as he broke away. One would have thought he was being asked to take the bloody dog for a walk.

In 'B' Flight, I was as usual flying Number 2 back up to 'Robin', who had the utter gall and temerity to break up a small formation of 109s on the way down, closing in behind the Dornier bombers. Unfortunately he misjudged the sweep in behind them and we clawed our way up the phalanx of bombers, trying to reach the leading formations where maximum break-up and confusion could be caused.

Our overtaking speed had been drastically reduced and we were literally flying above the backs of the Jerry bombers with the flank escort 109s much too close for anybody's comfort. I had been petrified earlier, but now I was shitting blue lights, at the sight of so many swastikas and black crosses. I was sticking like glue to 'Robin', waiting for his order to open fire, yet wishing like hell that he would call it off, and come back tomorrow, but 'Robin', bless him, pressed on.

Norman Ryder told me later that, as he saw us go in over the bombers, be offered up a little prayer for us, and a rapid farewell, as the flanking 109s swung in behind us. I was flying almost level with 'Robin' on his right as he gave the order to fire. The concentrated fire of sixteen Brownings ripped into the bombers which emitted clouds of smoke and bits of metal and broke formation as 'Robin' and I broke away rapidly to port, not waiting around to judge the results with 109s breathing down our necks. Shortly afterwards, I was able to attack a 109 without conclusive results.

Terry, following behind us in Blue section tried three times to get into position to attack the bombers, but was forced to break away by the harassing 109s behind him. 'A' Flight had been fully occupied with the 109 escorts and had done extremely well against the odds, the squadron being credited with quite a number of 109s confirmed and probable and the Dornier bombers, Robin and I had attacked, crashed at Calais and St Omer. The squadron were fortunate to suffer only slight damage to one Spitfire.

That afternoon an ill-fated interception nearly brought the squadron to it's knees. From the onset the feeling persisted that something was wrong. The hurried take-off was to intercept a large raid flying up the Thames Estuary at 15,000 feet composed of Heinkel 111 and Junkers 88 bombers with an escort of ME 109 fighters at high level top cover.

As usual I was flying Number 2 on 'Robin' Hood leading 'B' Flight and, being unable to gain height advantage and position in time, 'Robin' put us in line-astern and open echelon port and attacked head-on, a desperate manoeuvre that could age one very prematurely. Within seconds all hell broke loose and, as the action developed, 'B' Flight was overwhelmingly attacked by the 109s.

During this time the anti-aircraft defences were putting up a very accurate barrage on friend and foe alike, which, though disconcerting, gave comfort that someone down there wanted to help us.

Our flight formation broke up and, in the mêlée that followed, 'Robin' and Terry were believed to have collided, and did not survive. Lulu was hit but baled out uninjured. 'A' Flight had fared better, one pilot being slightly injured, for a good score of several German aircraft confirmed and probable.

After opening fire at the bombers coming so rapidly towards us, I had broken away violently and escaped the attacking 109s, diving vertically to 10,000 feet and climbing nearly as steeply back up sun. Turning, with the westering sun behind me, I searched for the action which, as ever, had moved away.

On a south-easterly heading, and jinking, I caught up with two 109s below returning home in open formation and, seeing no cover, attacked one with a long burst, which destroyed it. Then, like a foolish virgin, the most simple of novices, I committed the cardinal error and, instead of breaking violently away, slid across after the other 109.

As I lined the 109 up in my reflector sight the roof fell in on me, and I cursed the stupidity that would probably cost me my life. Of course, the Jerries were not fools, keeping a tail cover for protection, and I had fallen for it.

The 109, which I glimpsed screaming down had opened up, luckily at maximum range, and raked me with heavy and concentrated fire before I could move. The din was indescribable as the 109s cannon and machine gun fire tore great chunks out of my wings and blasted into the cockpit. My instrument panel disintegrated, my radio control disappeared, my armoured glass windscreen was scored on the inside but intact and my leg went numb with a hammer blow that, strangely, did not seem to hurt at all, as a cannon shell tore it apart.

The shock was so intense that I sat, unbelieving that I had been 'jumped' and must pay the forfeit, for what seemed ages, but really must have only been a moment before I reacted and broke away violently to port.

To my great relief the Spitfire recovered to straight and level flight, handling like a sack of coal. Looking at the havoc about me, I decided that my Spitfire was a most unhealthy place in which to linger. I had never previously baled out or done a parachute drop but this was no time to sit and weigh up the pros and cons.

The Spitfire 1 had no canopy jettison so I reached up to pull back the canopy and get out while the going was good. To my horror it would not budge and I realised that the burst of fire must have jammed it. I was sealed in and, slumping back in my seat, realised that the moment of truth had finally arrived.

How and when my sanity returned I do not know. A drowning man clutches at straws, and, shouting, more I think with desperate frustration than fear, I pulled myself together and tried to weigh up my chances of survival. I had to get the Spitfire down before the engine, which was labouring and clattering, blew up or went on fire.

Fortunately for me it did neither and I managed to head back towards Hornchurch, losing height and looking desperately for a field in which to crash land.

When within four miles of base the engine finally ground to a stop, at very low level. I had no choice but to put the aircraft down. My luck held as I rocketed across a field, smashed through a fence, hurdled a ditch like a Grand

National winner into another field, coming to rest in the shelter of a very large tree.

I sat there trapped in the cockpit for a hundred years or more until two men, running across the field, arrived to release me and help me out.

It was an astonishing thing but, during my noisy arrival, my attention was drawn to a hay-raking machine in the next field, the driver of which was having great difficulty in restraining his two terrified horses and I wanted to get out and apologise for being such a bloody nuisance.

CHAPTER 5

The End of the Beginning

It has been said that imminence of death gives added strength in the desperation to survive, but, no matter how desperately I hammered my fists against the jammed canopy, it was to no avail. I raised my seat to the top and frantically banged my helmeted head against the perspex, knowing that, if my petrol tanks had ruptured, the aircraft would, at any moment, go up in a frightful ball of fire. "Oh God, get me out, get me out," was all I could croak to myself in despair.

The two men running across the field were suddenly standing on the wing and I was yelling hoarsely at them to hit the button and prise the canopy back. I was dying by inches, trapped in suffocating heat with the will to live draining from me, when the seemingly freezing cold breeze of a hot afternoon wafted into the cockpit and strong hands were pulling at me to lift me out of my near-coffin. Some yards from the Spitfire I stood on one leg, supported by my two angels and tried, without success, hands shaking uncontrollably, to light a cigarette. My lovely Spitfire crackling like mad from its overheated and ruptured engine, lay forlornly on her belly under the tree. Cannon shells had gouged large chunks out of the top of the wings, shattered the rudder and smashed into the cockpit, reducing it to a shambles.

Later I found that one bullet had neatly removed my right radio ear-phone, from my helmet, another coming down through my sleeve had neatly removed the face from my wrist watch. But the most shattering news that day was that my back armour had been almost penetrated by cannon shells, still embedded in the metal, but just lacking the impetus to come through and split me apart, due, I imagine, to the toughness of the steel and the German who jumped me being just that fraction out of most effective range when he opened fire.

The men, whose names I never knew and who had saved my life, helped me to walk, as I belligerently refused to be carried, to their small car in the lane and drove me a short distance to a large building which they said was now a Hospital, at Orsett, just north of Tilbury on the River Thames.

Hospitals are full of ministering angels and men with healing hands. So, feeling very much under the weather and in need of a wash and brush up, I clenched my teeth and clambered, very painfully from the car, dishevelled, shirt and uniform soaked in sweat. I staggered into a small bare reception area, flanked by my two new-found friends and stood in front of a desk shouting 'Shop' and banging the desk-top. Looking round as we waited I saw a trail of blood from the door to a puddle at my feet and thought "What a bloody untidy bugger you are – you'll get hell for this."

A small slim nurse, who had obviously had a hard day too, came charging through the door and brusquely demanded "Yes, what is it?"

"I've called for some sticking plaster for my leg and a good stiff drink, please," I said and, with horror, heard myself adding, "and a cup of tea would be lovely."

The harassment of her day showed on her face as she said, in the same tone of voice, "Who are you, where are you from?"

Not being at my brightest and most courteous best at that moment, I mumbled, "I'm Wallens – RAF, just come down rather abruptly from Heaven and if you don't get a bloody move on I'm very soon on my way back up there," and pointed down to my leg where the trouser had disappeared exposing a ghastly mess of blood and mush.

I must have had a double ration of blood in my pipes that day or I should have passed out long before but I had the feeling that my dip-stick reading must be getting very low as the nurse merged into a haze and out of focus.

Bless her, she took one quick look and reacted without hesitation crying, "Sit him down, quickly" and rocketed to the door shouting, "Doctor, Doctor come quickly, hurry."

I never did get that cup of tea, though I remember a white-coated figure standing over me with a ten foot garden syringe in his hand which he was trying to ram into me as I resisted, shouting, "I can't stay, I've got to get back, I must get back, they'll want to know. For God's sake you must have a plaster or bandage or something," and then I knew no more.

He was standing over me again when I awoke, and holding my hand, which I found rather embarrassing, until he said something about my pulse, and let go. I was on a bed, the remnants of my trousers removed, with blood-soaked bandages covering my wound, and croaked feebly, "I could do with a drink – Doctor – even water will do, I'm parched."

"You've been very lucky, young man," he said, "whatever hit you has gouged a large chunk out of you. It's exposed but missed the leg bone by a fraction otherwise your leg would have to come off. As it is we have cleaned you up and will operate shortly and you'll be alright."

There I was, after a damnable day being told that I was lucky when the pain in my leg was now frighteningly intense, shooting and throbbing up through my body in spasms which were tearing me apart and, at that moment, I couldn't agree with him. In fact I told him to take the bloody thing off altogether, but he calmed me down, thank goodness.

The days following were a haze of pain with violent nightmares of noise, gunfire, the rending of metals and the smell of oil, glycol, blood and sweat in my nostrils. I felt desperately low and out of my own world, the world of tension, anticipation, apprehension, excitement, fear and sudden violence, which was now denied me, and I felt no sense of relief, luck, or good fortune that I had somehow walked away comparatively unscathed.

Yet, later, when sanity returned, I knew that my 'luck' was something that defied description or belief, as, by all the laws of average, I was 'due for the chop' when I took off that last afternoon.

As the days passed the tension eased, the frenetic urgency to get back in the fight diminished and I accepted that I must wait with patience until passed fit again for active duty.

I wrote to my mother telling her that I had had a slight mishap and that I was now where for years she had jokingly long predicted I should finish up – in the Workhouse and moreover, comfortably esconced in the Maternity Ward, to boot.

The hospital, previously a Workhouse, had been taken over by Barts, as London was now under attack, and I was the sole occupant of a smallish room with enough space for one bed, which says little for the procreative prowess of the previous occupants of the Workhouse.

It was only a few miles from my base at Hornchurch to which I was struggling to return before my Spitfire ran out of breath. Norman Ryder, my old friend of pre-war days in the Squadron, came to see me a few times and, while upbraiding me for being an idle, careless, clumsy clot who should not be entrusted with a rocking horse let alone a Spitfire, kept me up to date on how things were going. Norman was a great fellow, an extremely good pilot and tactician whose qualities of leadership and courage should have been more generously recognised. He later became POW during the offensives over France and survived the war.

Another pilot came to see me often, flying very low past my window, on his way home waving and waggling his wings. He was Johnny 'Beryl' Boyle, a short cheerful, laconic, Canadian who would perform the most hilarious antics with a 'dead-pan' expression that belied his wonderful sense of humour.

Missing the almost daily fly-past I casually asked Norman, on his next visit, if 'Beryl' had been posted to another squadron only to be told that another of the 'indestructibles' had finally 'bought it'. I felt so sad and helpless that I was not there.

I had been reduced to becoming a spectator as the battle raged above, jammed in a hard metal framed bed, my leg covered in plaster and a gooey dressing stinking of fish heads, but which, I was assured, was the right unction, although I had my doubts. My misery was made much worse by the news of more friends in the squadron being killed although the squadron was taking its toll of the enemy.

The Luftwaffe had begun large attacks on London itself and the battle raged until on the 15th September, when Fighter Command fought its most successful day battle which was the turning point of the whole Battle of Britain.

Hitler's prevarication on the decision to invade Britain was further continued by postponement to the 17 September and eventual abandonment two days later, and it is considered that Fighter Command's success against the 'invincible' Luftwaffe was probably the most telling factor.

In the House of Commons on the 20 August Winston Churchill had spoken the words, "Never in the field of human conflict was so much owed by so many to so few," a grand compliment to Fighter Command.

At Orsett time passed painfully and slowly, yet less painful after a while, as two medical students took to making evening calls for a game of poker. They were only too pleased to let me pay for a few bottles of sustenance and our soirées were a great success.

After a few months I was told that I was to be sent to Hill End Hospital, St Albans, for skin-grafting and that the American Red Cross would transfer me. Having persuaded Sister that parting is such sweeter sorrow if laced with gin or sherry I was permitted to set up a small farewell do, in my room, my student friends doing a remarkable job of obtaining the unobtainable.

My doctor, the staff, my two saviours from the crash, the students, the indestructible Norman Ryder and the two Red Cross nurses turned up promptly for a mid-morning kick-off and we had a most enjoyable party.

* * *

Having thanked and said goodbye to the nursing staff at the Hospital, all of whom had been so kind and considerate, we set off in a royal procession of an ambulance and two cars, ostensibly for St Albans. However, prior to leaving, a hastily convened bedhead committee meeting of the Wallens Welfare Group had unanimously voted in favour of a slight diversion from our course, in fact in the opposite direction, to the Orsett Golf Club. The American nurses, knowing prohibition had been repealed, fell in with the arrangement and the party, virtually intact moved to pastures new. I was on a stretcher and on arrival was placed on top of the bar, dressed for the occasion in a new pair of pyjamas of distinctive Russian origin, vivid red with black piping, a high collar, and a large Russian eagle or vulture emblazoned on the pocket.

The party was soon in full swing and the students suggested that we could do worse than a visit to Romford, which was roughly in the right direction and, there being no dissenters, we folded our tents and pressed on regardless.

On arrival it proved to be market day and crowded so we were directed to an upstairs bar to which I was carried in the near-vertical position clinging grimly to my stretcher which did everything but loop the loop. On the way down the stairs some time later I equalled the Cresta Run time for the one-man bobsleigh.

By this time it was about 4.30pm and time to head for St Albans so I said farewell to Norman and the students who were all that was left of those that had come under starter's orders. "Let us know when you're having another party like this," said some wag, which they all thought was very funny. A veil ought to be drawn over the next couple of hours.

Apparently I sat quietly in the back of the ambulance, unnoticed, swigging gently at a bottle which had been slipped under the blanket, as a parting gift.

On arrival at Hill End Hospital the evening was shattered by the firing of a revolver. On opening the ambulance doors, they saw me brandishing my revolver and an empty bottle, shooting at German paratroops who had, I insisted, landed on the roof of the ambulance.

* * *

Needless to say, I was taken away and put to bed, of which I recall nothing, and woke after a very long sleep, feeling like death, in a large ward, being inspected, quizzically and humorously by the other occupants. One of them, Pete, a handsome South Staffs Army Officer, badly wounded in the retreat to Dunkirk, said, "By the centre, that must have been some party. Going *out* in a blaze of glory, Yes, but coming *in*! Oh, Oh, Oh" and lay back and roared with laughter.

"What do you want, today Sir?" said a man dressed in an untidy raincoat topped by a trilby hat, at the foot of my bed.

I, ever polite, although rather fragile, replied, "Death, please, and no sugar." He smiled and waited for my next stupid remark. "What am I supposed to want?" I whispered to Pete, "Is he a surgeon or doctor?"

"Hell no, he's the fellow who brings our orders for grog and cigarettes from the town."

"Oh," I said, turning back to the bringer of good tidings, "I'll have a bottle of each and some Players, please." Which didn't appear to throw him, as he entered my order in his little book and departed.

I was in a large, pleasant ward, full of war-casualty officers of all Services, mostly bed-confined, being fussed over and scolded by a bevy of delightful nurses under the control of a very large imposing, stern-looking Sister, whom I later learned, in strict confidence, had been nicknamed 'Butterfly'. The ward was detached from, but connected by a long corridor, to the main hospital wards, a segregation, it had been suggested, to prevent any bad influence and habits, ie drink and cards, on the already long-suffering other ranks in the hospital, who, no doubt were already better qualified than all of us in such matters.

A little later Mr Mowlem, the senior surgeon visited the ward, and on inspecting my leg, had me booked down for an early operation, in preparation for skin-grafting. Having already had a couple of sessions in the operating theatre at Orsett I was, to say the least, most unenthusiastic, but gladly accepted his calm reassurances.

He was a charming man, a brilliant surgeon who daily performed remarkable feats of restoration of the shattered and burnt faces, bodies and limbs of those who had suffered so much more than I. I can recall the concentrated look of compassion and deep concern on his face when talking to hideously disfigured patients. I am sure that, had it been physically possible, he and his staff would have worked non-stop, day and night, without pause for sleep, food and drink, to lessen the pain of their charges.

Little did we know, but the horrors of war had followed us into the ward with blanket baths, the constant ritual of, "Nurse, bottle, please" then the daily soul-destroying, dignity-shattering performance of the bed-pan, the act that reduced strong men to gibbering travesties of humanity. If bravery, courage and valour in the heat of battle were required most men would not flinch, and press on to glory, but whisper "Enema" down the ward and one, even at death's door, would take up his bed and run like hell – not walk. Oh, happy days.

A spare bathroom at the end of the ward had, surreptitiously, been converted into a bar of sorts for the walking wounded. Every bedside locker was doing a roaring trade, particularly when one lay helpless in bed, a restricting metal cage over one's legs, staring helplessly up at the ceiling waiting. The Jerry bombers made their run across London that winter and with the ack-ack pounding away, dropped the odd few bombs very close to the hospital. Having a drink in bed is great fun, you just fall back and you're home and for all you care, for a moment at least, all the bloody Jerries can fall in the Thames and drown.

To relieve the monotony, McDonald of the Black Watch would give wheel-chair displays to a captive audience. He was, I consider the only man to master the art of solo-aerobatics in a wheel-chair, a virtuoso, and would come down the ward backwards, looking over his shoulder, propelling himself at a rate of knots, his gammy leg perched outright on a fracture board. With both hands revolving the wheels and his good leg, developed, by weeks of training into a bulging mass of sinew and muscle, pounding the floor for added impetus he gave a pre-Harrier exhibition of backward flying.

At centre stage he would clamp his hands on one wheel, locking it, lean inwards, and execute the most perfect pirouette, without moving from the spot, screeching some blood-curdling Highland War Cry that held us spellbound and applauding like mad.

Came the day when Mac announced that he had, in slower motion, perfected a double reverse pirouette, a figure of 8, and that he proposed to demonstrate with a high-speed run that evening, after we had taken a little nourishment before dinner.

All augured well as we asked 'Kipper', the Night Sister, to lower some lights for effect and, Olé Mac the Black Watch, the Highland Toreador, El Supremo of the wheel-chair, taxied up to the end of the ward. Pete, next to me, blew a fanfare, which sounded uncommonly like a 'raspberry' but politely ignored by Mac, hyping himself up on the end of the runway.

Mac bowed gravely from his mount, turned about and, without the slightest deviation, roared down the ward flat out, his arms and one leg a blur of superhuman effort. Features distorted, jaw out-thrust, the one-man Light Brigade thundered on.

Mac, beyond the point of no return, hit his brakes right on the button, pirouetted dizzily with the grace of Pavlova, reversed his engines to enter the truly unknown part of the manoeuvre, and suddenly performed an amazing, unrehearsed traverse at right angles, on one wheel, across the ward.

Jimmy, the One, a regular Naval Lieutenant, who had been blown off the bridge of his ship by a mine and suffered severe injuries to pelvis and legs, lay in a Pearson bed, spread-eagled in plaster and supports which were connected, for some reason, to pulleys and weights. With great aplomb and screaming, "Oh God, Man over board," Mac rammed the bed like a tank, rolled over and sprawled across the floor.

The Navy being the Navy, Jimmy the One had watched

the earlier performances with some little disdain – Junior service antics were rightly somewhat beneath his dignity. Imagine the Forth Bridge collapsing and that, in miniature, is what occurred.

The weights and pulleys took off in all directions and Jimmy was propelled down the bed until brought up by the bottom rail.

Sister went berserk, I suspect, primarily because like a knocked over chess game, it would be a problem to remember where all the bits went back. But I'm sure that the unexpected traction did Jimmy a power of good as he seemed much better when the smoke had cleared away.

Lying on my back, week after weary week, listening to the nightly drone of German bombers, the crump of exploding bombs and the incessant barking of the ack-ack guns, with intermittent painful operations, some of which, apparently, were unsuccessful and had to be repeated, skin-grafting being a slow process, made me fretful, impatient to return to the world at war, inexcusably impatient and rude to everyone. Yet they worked so tirelessly to restore health to physically damaged and mentally disturbed young men, knowing that they would be sending some of them back for a second, and often last, helping. I can only pay the highest tribute to them all, who merited so much more recognition for their wonderful work.

For some of my grafting, skin had been taken from my upper legs but after one particular operation I was put into a warm bath after the stitches had been removed from two large sticky gauze patches stuck to the cheeks of my bottom, where the skin had been taken and grafted to my leg.

I was told to ease the patches off in the warm water and, pulling gently, a little at a time, with a painful "Oh", and an "Ah" at each tug, the nerve ends being exposed, I think I could have removed the patches on my own in no time, say two or three weeks.

However, Mr Mowlem and 'Butterfly' came in to the bathroom where I was so busily and carefully engaged. "Morning Wallens, how goes it?"

"Fine Sir, thank you, it won't take long."

"Let me see," says he.

"Of course Sir" says I like a bloody fool, and rolled over.

No matter how complimentary I had been about surgeons and nursing staff prior to this moment I soon had bitter cause to regret and retract such statements. They are without doubt the most devious, uncaring, callous people in the whole world, taking fiendish delight in torture that makes the Inquisition's best efforts pale into insignificance by comparison.

Mr Mowlem and his accomplice, leaned over the bath. "Mm, what do you think Sister?" and she, with a barely disguised look of glee nodded sagely in agreement and before I could shout, "Tally-ho – Bandits at 12 o'clock" Mr M. had a dripping sheet of gauze in each hand, with I thought, momentarily, the whole of my backside attached. He had whipped them off in a flash in a movement that the eye could not register, like a triumphant magician lifting the cloth from a couple of twitching rabbits, although my bottom felt more like two skinned gophers.

I have a good instinct of anticipation and a sharp reaction and both have stood me in good stead, but, as it dawned on me, about 24 hours too late, what he was up to, the foul deed was done. If you should ever suddenly sit in a frying pan full of boiling, simmering fat you will get some idea of the feeling. I took off out of the bath, mouthing unprintable oaths, which I couldn't express as I sucked in my breath, the tears of shock running down my cheeks, higher than I have ever been before in a Spitfire.

"It's rather sad, but at times," said he, mildly, "One has to be a little cruel to be kind." I imagine he was right, they don't have much entertainment in their business and who was I to get stroppy and spoil their fun?

I was, in due course, allowed to go solo in a wheel-chair and fracture board and Mac, the torpedo artist, and I, to while away the time, organised a Head of the River event in the corridor from the main hospital down hill to our ward. We had cajoled a mixed bag of cripples like us to join in the fun and were set to 'scramble'.

This was a handicap race and planned meticulously on individual performance. Unfortunately some of the inexperienced novices made a hash of it. Mac, last to start, had passed me and was going like the proverbial rocket when he reached a blockage which he ploughed into and promptly sank, with all legs.

Apart from a few grazes, bent wheels and plaster cast chippings like a carpet of snow over the floor of the corridor, no serious damage was done. But what should appear on the scene at that moment, in full and imposing sail, but the Hospital Matron, with a shattering broadside. "You are all irresponsible children and should be sent home," which prompted loud and appreciative applause. Matron just hoisted more sail and, with great dignity and obvious disapproval, tacked majestically back up the corridor to her office.

Mac and I 'borrowed' some large stainless steel utensils swiped I think from the operating theatre, which were ideal for making prodigious quantities of Pimms, which we circulated round the ward until our cash and supplies ran out, so we approached the powers that be seeking permission to go down into St Albans to sample the local ale. Strangely, there was no opposition, other than the condition that we should return by 9.00pm and, in hospital, orders are orders.

The taxi driver arrived half an hour before opening time and, now being on crutches, with legs still in plaster, we were escorted out by the nurses and, under the solicitous direction of the driver, were eased gently into the taxi to cries of, "Ooh, mind my leg. Take care there, Ooh, Aah" etc and were unloaded just as carefully to the pavement outside our chosen hostelry as the doors of Valhalla opened. We were made most welcome there, arranging our legs perched on stools at the bar spending a very pleasant evening and enjoying a chat with the locals. When time was up we left the pub for the return journey but, once outside, found the taxi driver a very changed man, or we were oblivious to his changed tactics.

I think he wanted to get somewhere to a warm fire or a warmer blonde, as he grabbed us, one at a time, and with a cheerful, "Heave-ho, me hearties", rammed us into the taxi one at a time like sides of beef, ignoring the gentle remonstrations of, "Mind my bloody leg, you great oaf," "Christ you've knackered my plaster." "Don't ram that crutch up my backside, you clot," and others less printable, slammed the door and drove us home.

Staggering from the taxi, a good whip-round for the driver and we weaved on our crutches in line-astern into the ward where the highly-polished floor, and 'Kipper', the night sister waited to bring about our downfall. If wheels had been fitted to each pair of crutches the effect could not have been more spectacular, as each of us strove valiantly to negotiate the 'ice-rink' and came an unholy purler to moans of anguish and pain, muffled curses and the usual light fog of lacerated plaster adding an enchanting back-drop to the last entertainment of the day.

One could not but be deeply affected by the courage of some of the fellows in the ward who, uncomplainingly, lay in agony day after day, with the lines of pain so deeply etched into their drawn, white faces. Often one could not stand by their beds and look into their eyes for fear of betraying one's feelings.

But it is remarkable how the spirit in man to surmount

adversity can shine through at times, and often in the most unusual ways.

John, an Army Officer, had been wounded in the fighting in France and had been brought home through Dunkirk. His injuries included damage to his face and the loss of one eye.

Eventually he was a walking case and, wearing a piratical eye patch, would join us in the trips down to St Albans for our usual light refreshment. He was very conscious of his facial scars and appearance and, understandably, could not relax, particularly when he caught the sidelong glances of the curious in the bar.

He was sent up to London for the fitting of a new glass eye and, on his return, we all inspected and marvelled at the new orb which, matching his other good one perfectly, stared unwinkingly at us.

We had expected an improvement in his manner but, after two more visits to St Albans with us, the second of which ended up in an hilarious party, he seemed morose to the point of morbidity and, early the next morning rose early without speaking to anyone, dressed and left the hospital.

Two evenings later we were as usual, at the seat of alcoholic custom in St Albans, and just warming up when in came a rejuvenated John. Not the sad, miserable chap we knew but a different man with an unbelievable gleam in his glass eye with which he proceeded to put on a well-rehearsed exhibition.

Starting with us, he stood and glared at everyone, turned aside and, in a flash, flicking his hand across his face, turned back and was looking at us with his glass eye peering out of the corner of its socket and again, in a flash and it was peering upwards, downwards and then finally squinting across the bridge of his nose in the most exaggerated an comical cock-eyed, cross-eyed fashion that had all screaming with laughter.

During the evening John demonstrated his artistry to some of the locals, some of whom were highly amused, others, thinking it was all a bit much, being unable to feel and understand the emotions that prompted his actions.

He went to the loo, returning to the bar a few minutes later and stood before us again and this time it was his pièce de résistance, as we stood speechless and open-mouthed as he explained. "After I got this bloody great snooker ball I just couldn't stand it staring at me in the shaving mirror in the morning when my good one looked so ragged after the night before, so I went up to London and persuaded the eye man to make me another for mornings. How do you like it?"

It was a masterpiece, a work of art. Beady, bleary, mottled and red-veined it stared dully at us, the epitome of the effect of a good hangover.

We cheered him to the echo, plied him with a modicum of lotion until his good eye had deteriorated to the same matching condition and took him happily home.

His last remark was "If we have many more parties like this I think I shall have to put the snooker ball away for the duration," and we knew that John's sense of humour had risen to the occasion.

* * *

Shortly after my arrival at Hill End a young pilot named Robin had been placed on my other side in the ward and my first sight of the terrible burns he had suffered when shot down made me want to get up and run away in horror.

He had been a very good looking young chap but now his face was hideously disfigured, the nose and mouth unrecognisable yet his eyes held mine in a steady gaze and I could feel his sympathy for me, watching my face which betrayed me.

Mr Mowlem had kept Robin away in a separate ward for a long while as he did the preliminary surgical preparation prior to major skin grafting and told us it was time for Robin to join us in the main ward, so I dread to think how he had looked when he first came in to hospital.

His hands also had suffered terribly with some of the fingers burnt away and the remainder virtually immobile, but he would struggle, uncomplaining, without a murmur, to eat his food or play a game of cards.

Robin endured innumerable small, painful graftings but the major operation to rebuild his face was carried out in several remarkable stages. In the first the skin on his chest was cut in two vertical lines about eight to ten inches long, two to three inches apart, and the skin, still attached at each end, lifted away to form a 'handle'. The next operation was to sever one end and attach it to his upper face and, afterwards, the other end was severed and attached to his chin, so he had a live strip of skin ready to be spread out across his face.

Meanwhile Mr Mowlem had rebuilt the structure of his nose ready for the final operation, which when finished was a remarkable transformation and a great success, although Robin would suffer a disfigurement that could never be erased, the scars remaining for ever.

Our favourite patient improved terrifically and, although partially bandaged about the head, and hands, was allowed up. Mr Mowlem, aware of our evening trips to St Albans, suggested that it would do Robin a power of good to join us in public, to which we heartily agreed. It took a very great deal of persuasion by ourselves and Mr Mowlem, to get Robin to come with three of us to the Pea Hen, in St Albans, a pleasant, quiet hotel in the town.

I suppose that the familiar sight of Robin was acceptable to us, although to strangers could be somewhat of a shock, but I was not prepared for what followed as we walked through the lounge to the bar. A woman, seated in the lounge with friends, took one look at Robin and said in a very loud voice "It's disgusting, they should not allow Service people out looking like that and the hotel should not let them in. Disgraceful."

Robin was some way ahead and, I prayed to God, had not heard the callous remark as he disappeared into the bar. I whirled about on my crutches and, I think, white with fury, addressed her harshly. "Madam, this War has brought death and suffering to many young men. We have suffered a little but that young man has suffered the most terrible burns one can imagine and at last, has the courage to face the world again for the first time and you would deny him the chance to live again. I only hope that if you have a son and he should ever, God forbid, stand before you in the same condition you may have the guts to show the same lack of compassion and may it rest on your conscience. Damn you, Damn you." I wanted to curse her and use all the filthy words I could conjure up but I could feel the bitter tears for Robin welling up in my eyes and stumbled blindly to the toilet to regain my composure before Robin could see me, and guess the truth.

* * *

Many months had passed and came the time in the late Spring of 1941 when it was considered that the skin-grafting to my leg had taken satisfactorily, although still weeping and requiring daily dressings. My ankle was virtually immobile but I was able to get about at a slow gallop.

I had requested, and was instructed, to return to my squadron at Hornchurch, and said my farewells to Mr Mowlem and those wonderful hospital staff at Hill End, who, despite our grouchy bad-tempered irritable black moods and childish behaviour, had never spared themselves to get us back to health and good spirits.

I knew I had been away too long. I wanted, desperately, to fly again with 41 Squadron, but was full of apprehension as I travelled across London to Hornchurch, hobbling with a walking stick, my leg throbbing with a constant ache and my ankle feeling like a car's seized-up wheel-bearing, not giving with each painful step.

A feeling possessed me that I was going back to something for which I was not prepared. I was alone, on the Underground, and the noise and the flashing lights conjured up visions I couldn't accept. I was fearful that, at the end of my journey, it could all happen again, and this time, with much more pain and misery and I recoiled from the frightful picture I saw.

To make it worse, it was a terribly sad return, with so many familiar faces missing and only my old friends, Norman Ryder, Lulu Lovell and Mac Mackenzie left to greet me. They, ever cheerful, ragged me and did their best to make me welcome.

The pilots of the squadrons, who stood around in the Ante Room in the Mess having a tankard of beer, were different, with a new set of expressions and attitudes, a new race taking up the sword from those that had gone, luckily with a few wise old heads left to guide them. I could sense their side-long glances at an 'old' man limping about with a stick, and they wanted no reminder that war was for the quick and the dead, and not for a 'clobbered' cripple.

I felt completely out of touch, as in a dream, and more despondent than ever, breaking out in a cold sweat as I knew that I could not, as yet, go through it all again. With an over-sensitivity, which I would deny I ever possessed, I shied from trying to talk to anyone, although I am sure they were sympathetic and would have done their best to put me at ease. I suppose I was being too reactive, returning too quickly to the place where so much had happened and where vivid memory rose no matter how hard I tried to close the shutters of my mind.

My visit next morning to the dispersal to meet the CO, Donald Finlay, and squadron pilots was a disaster. I was totally inarticulate and must have appeared a most miserable, uncommunicative wretch. The Spitfires stood silent, watchful, mutely beckoning me to climb in, take off and tear down the river again to meet the swarms of German bombers and fighters roaring up the Estuary, but which were now long gone.

I don't know what held me in such tension. It wasn't fear – that, as best one can, I had mastered long before – but I felt fragile, brittle, lost, and with a frightening apprehension that something terrible would happen to me if I stayed.

(Later at the RAF convalescent hospital at Torquay the senior Medical Officer calmly allayed this gnawing, destroying, traumatic misery that held me, and helped me to regain a clearer view).

However, my future was quickly decided for me when the Medical Officer inspected my weeping leg and promptly sent me up to London for further examination. I was told that despite my request I should not have been sent back to Hornchurch again. I was not fit to fly, and it was most unlikely that I would ever again be given a full category for operational flying. I was to be sent to the RAF convalescent hospital in the Palace Hotel, Torquay for an indefinite period.

41 (Fighter) Squadron.

Formed in 1916. Badge composed of red double-armed cross from the Town Arms of St Omer, where the squadron had it's first overseas Headquarters in the 1914/18 War, in which it served with distinction.

The Motto of 41 Squadron – "SEEK AND DESTROY"

For the last time I left Hornchurch, bidding goodbye to Norman, Lulu and Mac, the only remains of the 41 Squadron I had known so well and so long, knowing that I should never be fully fit to fly again in one of the finest front-line fighter squadrons, and I felt bloody awful.

CHAPTER 6

Through a Glass – darkly

During the months that I had lain abed in hospital, immobile, in pain and continual discomfort, and low-hearted at the prospect of many more empty days to follow, I had ample time to reflect on events since that 11 o'clock radio broadcast on the 3rd of September so many months, or was it years?, before.

The 'Phoney' War had given way to the blitzkrieg sweep across Europe of the victorious German forces, and the rapid collapse of armed resistance ending in the Dunkirk evacuation, leaving Britain bravely and defiantly alone.

The success of Fighter Command in the Summer and Autumn of '40 in shattering and halting the massive daylight air attacks by the Luftwaffe on southern England, forcing cancellation of the imminent German invasion plans, had brought the urgent respite needed by a Britain reeling a little against the ropes of the arena of conflict.

Although the British people were to suffer hideous casualties in further heavy day and night bombing of London, the major cities, industrial and 'open' targets, and had listened to and read nothing but depressing reports of defeats and disasters, they had been stirred by the speeches of the Prime Minister, Winston Churchill, and I quote –

> "What General Weygand called the Battle of France is over. I expect that the Battle of Britain is about to begin. The whole fury and might of the enemy must very soon be turned on us. Hitler

knows that he will have to break us in this island or lose the War. If we can stand up to him, all Europe may be free and the life of the world may move forward into broad sunlit uplands. But if we fail, then the whole world, including the United States, including all that we have known and cared for, will sink into the abyss of a new Dark Age made more sinister, and perhaps more protracted, by the lights of perverted science. Let us therefore brace ourselves to our duties, and so bear ourselves that, if the British Empire and its Commonwealth last for a thousand years, men will still say, this was their finest hour."

(18th June 1940)

"I would say to the House, as I said to those who have joined this Government, I have nothing to offer but blood, toil, tears and sweat."

(13th May 1940)

"We shall defend our island, whatever the cost may be, we shall fight on the beaches, we shall fight on the landing grounds, we shall fight in the fields and in the streets, we shall fight in the hills; we shall never surrender."

(4th June 1940)

"The gratitude of every home in our Island, in our Empire, and indeed throughout the world, except in the abodes of the guilty, goes out to the British airmen who, undaunted by odds, unwearied in their constant challenge and mortal danger, are turning the tide of World War by their prowess and by their devotion.

Never in the field of human conflict was so

much owed by so many to so few."

(20th August 1940)

Churchill's ability to generate and instil his calm, unwavering confidence was well demonstrated on the 15th September.

The air battles on that day had reached an unbelievable crescendo of intensity and ferocity, the Luftwaffe throwing in wave after wave of attackers in a last desperate attempt to subdue the RAF. Air Vice Marshal Park had virtually no reserves on which to call but the British line held firm and that day was to be the turning point. Goering was to confess, "We'd forgotten that the English fight best with their backs to the wall."

Churchill in his study until very late into the night, at last left to take a little rest and, seeing his personal guard Inspector Walter Thompson standing there in utter fatigue, expressed his concern. "You're exhausted Thompson," he said putting his arm round the man's shoulder, and when poor Thompson agreed, continued, "We're going to win, you know, it will be worth it in the end," and, still with his arm around the man's shoulder, walked him slowly down the corridor.

The nation had responded to his Shakespearean histrionics, shaking off the earlier lethargy and the attitudes of 'too little, too late', which for too long had been the cry, applying itself to the resurgence of a new spirit of survival and ultimate victory, no matter how long, hard and weary the road.

Personally, I had been more than relieved when the news of the cancellation of the intended invasion was confirmed. From my first day in hospital my service revolver had been my constant bed companion, despite the exhortations, pleadings and direct threats of the doctors and staff.

The civilian population had keyed themselves up to resist invasion by whatever means came to hand, the oft-ridiculed 1914 rifles, shotguns, pikestaffs and even clubs against the most efficient, ruthless and deadly army ever assembled. Mercifully, they were unaware of the probable response of the German Army, which would be predictably harsh and unmerciful, and more particularly of the special forces of the Gestapo and SS trained to commit the most ruthless and terrible mass murders and wholesale atrocities that evil minds can devise.

These units would have removed all the political, civic and intellectual leaders, transported all men of military age and then set up mass-murder squads in every major city to purge every conceivable organisation which might be considered as non-co-operative, such as the Church, Trade Unions, Jews, Masons, public schools and even the boy scouts. None would be spared.

Any para-military or civilian resistance would be ruthlessly crushed and military personnel temporarily hospitalised, like myself, would have been eliminated. The subjugation of the British people would be total, complete, without any mercy, more professional, fearful and terrifying than any invader anywhere had ever previously perpetrated.

I also had accepted the belief held by many that, in the event, there could be no compromise and the sardonic slogan, "You can always take one with you" would be our epitaph, but felt a relief tinged with hilarity at Churchill's calm reassurance to the French people on 21 October 1940, "We are waiting for the long promised invasion – so are the fishes."

From the early Summer of 1940 our squadron had been heavily engaged, coming through with flying colours but sadly, like many others, losing so many of the 'old hands' and a lot of 'new kids' on the way.

The Luftwaffe, designed as a formidable tactical air

component, had to fight the Battle of Britain as a battle of strategy, dictated by our Commander in Chief, ACM Dowding, ably assisted by his Group Commanders in the tactical field.

Hermann Goering, Commander in Chief of the Luftwaffe, and his senior commanders, had little knowledge of the strategic application and deployment of their forces and, being too inflexible in their thinking, under-estimated the capabilities of the RAF.

Fighter Command formed under the command of Dowding in 1936 had been honed to a fine sharpness and was thus able to implement Dowding's preconceived plans on the defence of Great Britain.

The clash of the mighty Luftwaffe, superior in numbers and experience, and the few squadrons of Fighter Command, mainly over southern England had raged through the summer months into autumn with increasing fury and intensity, until at last Hitler cried 'enough' and the Luftwaffe called a halt to the massive daylight raids, defeated in their attempt to crush the RAF and pave the way for the invasion of England.

For the first time, and probably the last, an aerial war had taken place in a set-piece of attack and defence and had been fought to a bloody and decisive conclusion. Yet the 'fighter boys' were, in the main, unaware at the time of the full significance of the battle, but satisfied that they were giving of their best, and would not back down.

The only time there was slightest doubt, misgiving or apprehension amongst us occurred when there was news that, if the situation justified it, meaning, of course, imminent invasion, the Royal Family and the Cabinet would be evacuated to Canada.

This was a stark reminder to emphasise the danger that England faced, met by a strong reaction of determination to fight to the bitter end.

That Air Chief Marshal Dowding was the right man to wield Fighter Command, there can be no doubt. That Air Vice Marshal Park was the right man to command 11 Group, backed up by AVM Brand in 10 Group, there can be no doubt. But, no-one could conceive of the dramatic events that were to unfold in November 1940 when the Battle was won, a shameful episode in the history of the Royal Air Force.

The victorious commanders, ACM Dowding, Air Officer commanding Fighter Command and AVM Keith Park AOC 11 Group were almost summarily relieved of their commands, Dowding being retired and sent on a tour of the United States, and asked to do various jobs that were an insult to his status, Park being sent to run a training group, actions that sent shock waves of disbelief throughout Fighter Command.

The seeds were sown in 1936, when Dowding, as Air Member for Supply and Research was appointed AOC-in-C Fighter Command, despite the opposition of senior RAF Commanders. He was a man apart, withdrawn, aloof, dedicated to the task of the air defence of Britain, making few friends and many enemies in high places. His idealism, to ensure that nothing but the best was good enough, overriding opposition that would seek his eventual downfall, was to be his Achilles heel.

The dissensions that had beset his path through the years finally came to a head in the Summer of 1940. Park, as Commander of 11 Group, had of necessity to call on the adjoining Groups for back up and assistance in the deployment of fighter cover. AVM Brand AOC 10 Group was ever ready to comply, but a situation had arisen between Park and AVM Leigh Mallory AOC 12 Group which developed into violent disagreement and personal enmity.

Leigh Mallory leaned towards offence tactics, considering

the 'Big Wing' (a formation of three to six squadrons) as the weapon to repel the large raiding Luftwaffe formations. Park, a brilliant defence tactician considered the 'Big Wing' as unwieldy, time-wasting and not a flexible defence unit but an attack unit, for which the circumstances were not applicable. Most of the fighter pilots agreed completely with him.

The enmity between the two became a bitter hatred as Leigh Mallory's obsession with the 'Big Wing' led to occasions when requested support was too late, or not at all, particularly when cover was required for 11 Group's Spitfires and Hurricanes to land and refuel after interceptions and the 'Big Wing' was not in place to provide this but looking for the enemy down the Thames Estuary or beyond.

Dowding was unaware of the difficulties that Park was encountering with Leigh Mallory, and which he had endeavoured to resolve alone. When the time came for Dowding to intervene it was too late – for both of them.

Douglas Bader, the legless CO of 242 Squadron at Duxford, had been one of the instigators of the 'Big Wing' theory, long favoured by Leigh Mallory and, freely critical of the current fighter attacks and tactics operated by 11 and 10 Groups, sought to promote his theory.

He was supported by his adjutant Peter Macdonald, a Member of Parliament, who gained the ear of the Under Secretary of State for Air and of Winston Churchill, and Leigh Mallory had the endorsement of Air Chief Marshal Sholto Douglas, Deputy Chief of the Air Staff, and Archibald Sinclair.

Despite overwhelming odds, the brilliant strategy of Dowding had been sustained and the tactical operation by Park of his 11 Group squadrons had been successful. The introduction of 'Big Wing' tactics, in the earlier phases would have been disastrous and the Luftwaffe would have been victorious.

But the long-standing resentments and jealousies in high places in the Air Ministry were developing into devious attempts to undermine and belittle Dowding's actions, and the protagonists of the Wing doctrine were going to remarkable lengths to bring about the downfall of both Dowding and Park.

At one Staff meeting Park was criticised for his handling of the Battle, and Bader, a junior officer, a Squadron Leader, was called in by Leigh Mallory to express his views, an unprecedented and unjustified situation.

At a subsequent meeting Dowding and Park received little recognition for their efforts, Park, in particular, receiving only brickbats. The outcome had already been decided and Dowding was retired to make way for Air Chief Marshal Sholto-Douglas as AOC-in-C, Fighter Command, and, to add insult to injury, Leigh Mallory took command of 11 Group from the embittered Park.

The irony of the whole damning, devious, surgical operation, that had been so foully perpetrated on two such brilliant and dedicated men, was the vindication of Park's tactical theories in 1941, when Leigh Mallory attempted to carry out a paper exercise based on a specific air battle incident in September 1940, but using the 'Big Wing' tactic. The exercise was a dismal failure.

Two years later Park, commanding the air defence of Malta, was to use almost identical tactics to those employed so successfully in 1940 to repulse the enemy and, once more, confound his critics.

Following the removal from their posts of Dowding and Park, Winston Churchill, who once described the 'fighter boys' as Dowding's 'chicks' because of his overwhelming concern for their welfare, and who must have been aware of the intrigues, was later to react with a furious outburst to the Air Minister on seeing the Air Ministry booklet on the Battle of Britain which made no reference to Dowding. "The jealousies and cliquism which have led to the committing of this offence are a discredit to the Air Ministry . . . What would have been said if . . . the Admiralty had reported the Battle of Trafalgar and left Lord Nelson out of it?"

That such a remarkable and distinguished man as Dowding, who deserved so much, wanted nothing and, sadly, received so little, could quietly accept his dismissal without rancour or petty recrimination is the hallmark of his greatness. His aloofness, so in contrast to the rakish, couldn't-care-less attitude of the pilots he commanded had prompted them to give him the nickname of 'Stuffy', a title, in the British tradition, which belied the respect and admiration in which he was held.

I close this part of the story with remarks made by some of the pilots on hearing Winston Churchill's commendation "Never in the field of human conflict was so much owed by so many to so few," comments which reflect the British spirit and say it all.

> *Hugh Dundas*: "I suppose we were all quite proud when we heard that. But I also suppose we thought it was a bit of a joke. We didn't take that sort of thing very seriously."

> *James Storrar*: "We'd had our baptism of fire over Dunkirk and had taken a terrible beating in the south. We were up in Scotland recuperating when we heard about that speech by Churchill. We thought, "Aren't they brave chaps down there and thank God we're not there?"

> *Robert Doe*: "It was the first time I realised that we might have done something unusual. I hadn't realised it until then."

> *Al Deere*: "We'd had a hellish day. When I heard

about what Churchill said about the many and the few, I said to my friend George Gribble – he was killed in action later – 'By Christ, he can say that again. There aren't many of us left'."

And lastly, the classic 'crack' attributed to an anonymous pilot with a superlative sense of humour – "I thought he was talking *about our Mess Bills!*"

For what it is worth I add a postscript.

By Jean Paul Richter (1763-1825)
(Quoted by Carlyle)

"Providence has given to the French the Empire of the land, to the English that of the sea, and to the Germans *that of the air.*"

<u>But not over England in 1940 – NOT BLOODY LIKELY</u>

Wally Wallens

From the outbreak of War in September 1939 until I was shot down in September 1940 I, like the other squadron pilots remaining, had been, with very few breaks, on constant readiness, flying on occasion from dawn till dusk, in all weathers, maintaining interminable patrols and being involved in many interceptions and combats. I thought I had been very lucky indeed to record nearly 200 hours of operational flying without getting 'clobbered'.

Like many other fighter pilots, who had pressed home their attacks, but had no confirmation of successes, I knew that I had destroyed, or damaged beyond survival, more than double the number of German aircraft for which I had been given credit. We accepted such decisions with good grace, very few seeing individual success in a tally of 'kills' as being of more importance than the eventual outcome – victory against the Luftwaffe.

CHAPTER 7

Pranks at the Palace

Convalescence at the Palace Hotel at Torquay was a minor extension of hospital life and the strength in my leg slowly returned although the wound would not dry up and gave a lot of discomfort. With a stick I hobbled about reasonably happily, but with impatience to get back to flying again.

There I met an old friend who had joined the Service with me at Perth in the very early days and had recently crash-landed and suffered a broken leg.

Frankie Scragg was a short, blonde character, with a permanent grin on his face, a very obvious enjoyment of life, and an uncanny and unerring ability to step the wrong side of authority.

He had, at FTS joined me in the escapade of changing seats in the Audax in mid-air and was always ready to try anything once, twice, or three times.

We were permitted the privilege of the 'penny a week' bus, a mini coach service laid on through the kindness of local people subscribing to a daily bus service for us to Torquay and back to the Palace at certain times of day, normally returning on its last trip about 9.30 pm just when the evening was warming up in the town, particularly at the Imperial and the Queens Hotels. We would stay there late and get a taxi back, the only problem then being the means of getting into the Palace, unseen by the Night Sister in reception.

There were two options, dependent on the agility and

fitness state of the late-comer, either up the fire escapes and in through a back window, or down the coal chute and up the stairs.

This worked well in the main if one were properly briefed. At breakfast one morning a newcomer was asked by another more recent newcomer, "My God, your face, what a mess, what happened, Flak?" "Not bloody likely" said the other "I'm only here for a hernia but I was badly briefed and came down the coal chute head first by mistake and stuck my face into the coal heap at the bottom at high speed."

However, Frankie and I had evolved a routine of staying on at the Queens when there was a dance. Frankie soon became very popular with the band as he had an amazing musical ability. Though completely untrained musically, he could play the piano reasonably well and the drums like Gene Krupa, the legendary American drummer. His 'turn' brought roars of applause and of course we were asked to have a drink and meet girls and more drinks and meet more girls.

Until one evening when we stayed on to the very end of the dance and tried to get a taxi or a lift back to the Palace. That evening we were out of luck and stood on the harbourside outside the Hotel praying for a miracle.

As nothing happened I said, "Frankie, we walk back".

"How the hell can we walk back, I'm on two sticks and you're on one," he replied.

"Well," said I, "I'm fitter than you so I'll carry you."

Easier said than done, as we set off up the Babbacombe Road, Frankie luckily very slim and light, perched on my back and we must have gone at a spanking pace as, after nearly two hours, we were nearly at the top, and had covered at least half a mile.

By this time I had, after several stops to rest, removed my

tunic and tie, and was in a state of near collapse, my leg throbbing like mad, while Frankie was crooning softly to himself and enjoying the upper deck view.

Staggering along, the Ancient Mariner with the Old man of the Sea perched atop, we crested the rise and it was all downhill from then on. Eventually, some days later it seemed, we swung into the Palace drive with the band playing, the skirl of pipes, the banging of the bass drum the clash of cymbals and a trail of perspiration running down my back and legs like the Niagara Falls.

"Good evening, gentlemen; my, my, if it isn't Mr Scragg and Mr Wallens, out for a little stroll are we?" was the solicitous sarcastic greeting from the Night Sister. By this time dawn was breaking.

"Oh for Christ's sake Sister, good morning, goodnight and a merry bloody Christmas as well" said I as I slipped Frankie from my back and collapsed into a chair. "And bring out your bloody firing squad as well, if it pleases you."

Expecting the worst, a black report in the book and a subsequent rocket, we were amazed, when the Sister produced two cups of tea and cigarettes and said, "I can't report you for being late back last night which was yesterday, but I will commend you for being such early risers today to take exercise to hasten your convalescence." There the matter ended, as she shepherded us to bed.

Dan Maskell, the 'King' of Wimbledon and one of the nicest persons one could ever meet, was in charge of the physical rehabilitation of patients in the gymnasium on the lower floor, where we were put through agonising sessions of therapy. I was glad that he escaped the murder that we, the suffering patients, wished to mete out to him when we were made to force unwilling limbs and muscles to return to some form of normal function.

I suggested to Dan that it would be nice if we could take

dinghies from Torquay across to Brixham for some fresh air and exercise (not to mention a skin-full of ale, and piles of fresh crab sandwiches) to which he readily agreed, and we hired four dinghies from Torquay Harbour and set sail. The Pilgrim Fathers had nothing on us for navigation, although we almost went past Berry Head and out into the Atlantic.

The trip was a great success except for one smart-arse idiot, and there's always one at every party. Sailing back gently to Torquay full of beer and bonhomie we took it in turns to lay off at the harbour entrance and come in to the inner harbour under minimum sail to arrive at the steps to tie up.

The loud-mouthed nautical genius decided that, coming in, deliberately last, he would give a display of sailing technique for us peasants to appreciate and applaud. We stood on the quayside as he came through the harbour entrance, partially closed by a blockship sunk in the entrance, and, under full sail headed for the steps.

Unfortunately, he left the lowering of his sail too late or it stuck, and doing about ninety knots he roared into the inner harbour. The dinghy hit the base of the steps, disintegrated and sank. As our hero floundered in the water we applauded to the echo and after doing a fair imitation of the service of Burial at Sea strolled along the harbourside to the Queens Bar.

Frankie and I arrived at the Queens one evening and as usual joined the crowd in the back bar having a pint or two but could find nowhere to park our greatcoats. Unknown to us one of our inmates had been rigged out in a metal contraption attached around his waist, with an outrigger supporting his arm above his shoulder in a near-Nazi-saluting position with his plastered fist clenched about the upper framework.

Quick to react to the possibility that the Germans had invaded and not wishing to be impolite or lacking in military courtesy, Frankie and I clicked our heels to attention threw up our arms in a mock Nazi salute crying, "Sieg heil, heil Hitler" and grabbing our greatcoats, hung them on this heaven-sent coat rack.

The poor chap stood for a moment, upright with his pint in his other hand and then under the weight slowly keeled over and went an almighty purler on the floor. We picked him up, dusted him off and straightened one of the supports, the wrong way which didn't help, but despite a yelp of agony all he said was, "What a bloody good idea, but please give me a little warning next time, chaps, you've spilt my ale." So of course we bought him another.

Having honestly described and admitted my feelings about returning to Hornchurch from Hill End Hospital to the Senior Medical Officer at Torquay, he very patiently, and at length, discussed the matter with me, although I cannot express or describe the medical terms and descriptions involved.

It would appear that, in simple terms, my mind and body would not back me up in my desire to get back to the Squadron at Hornchurch. I was at a psychological crossroads. No matter how often I said I must get back there they contradicted me, putting my head in turmoil and my leg, strangely, in a state where the weeping only worsened.

I had been told to relinquish all thought or intention of returning to Hornchurch now or ever and I did my best to comply. It sounds ridiculous but, after a few weeks at Torquay, my head cleared and I could think clearly once more, without getting the bouts of depression and misery.

The condition of my leg improved enormously and, although 'weeping' at intervals for several years afterwards, has only occasionally given me the terrible pain that had gnawed at me before.

Again came the day when goodbyes had to be said and this time without the sorrow. In the summer of 1941 I left

Torquay, being posted to Hendon.

Sad to relate, some weeks later I was informed that my old friend Frankie Scragg had returned to flying and tragically lost his life in a flying incident.

CHAPTER 8

No. 1 A.D.F. Hendon and Croydon

My cup, if not overflowing, was up to the plimsoll line with the elixir of life, the potent, heady stimulant I needed so badly – I was being returned to flying again and all was very well with my world.

I had been granted a limited, non-operational flying category and, expecting to be posted to Training Command for flying instruction duties, was pleasantly surprised to be told to report to No. 1 Aircraft Delivery Flight, Hendon. I was still in Fighter Command and, more particularly, in 11 Group, and could not ask for more.

Leaping Lena II

RAF Hendon, just north of London, off the Edgware Road, with Colindale Tube conveniently at the door, had been a renowned pre-War Station, where the major air displays were held and also headquarters of the City of London Auxiliary Air Force Squadrons. It was currently occupied by No. 24 Communications squadron, a large unit which operated the aircraft and duties of the King's Flight and transport of VIPs and senior officers.

Much later, after the war, the Station became the permanent site of the Royal Air Force Museums. The magnificent large display area incorporated the Bomber Command and Battle of Britain Museums, and a visit there must be a top priority when one is in London.

The prosaic, unimaginative and unexciting title of my new unit, No. 1 ADF belied the importance and responsibilities for which it was established and which at that time appeared to be taken in a most off-hand, haphazard manner.

It was the largest of four air ferry units throughout the country, responsible for the movement of replacement and exchange fighter and other aircraft in Fighter Command within the UK, using 8-10 seater twin-engined DH 89 Dominie (Rapide), and odd light aircraft, for transporting pilots.

A daily flood of urgent telephone calls and postagrams from Fighter Command HQ provided ample employment for the dozen or so pilots in the unit, all of varying lack of ability and enthusiasm, some, like myself, were of limited medical category through combat. Others were swinging the lead with coughs, colds, inflammation of the bladder, hernia, piles, and phantom pregnancies. I was not very impressed.

It was an important and very essential job, but being run on a nine to five basis and closed to customers at weekends. I felt there was a hell of a lot of room for improvement, which I was able to put into practice 'ere long when I took command of the unit.

Meanwhile, I was happy to renew my acquaintance with Spitfires and Hurricanes, brushing up on my rusty cross-country navigation and flying any odd or unusual aircraft that were carelessly left lying unattended.

All our flying, including that of the transport aircraft, was done without the benefit of radio aids or homing facilities. The aircraft being ferried were never fully equipped to squadron requirements when collected new from Maintenance units and, if collected from a squadron, would never have the required on-going radio frequencies and, sometimes, not even a radio set. As each of the transport aircraft had to make several calls each day, dropping off and collecting pilots at different airfields, it was impossible to operate radio communication. All flights had to be carried out under VFR (Visual Flight Rules), map-reading, often below very low cloud and minimal visibility conditions.

The variety of aircraft required to be flown ranged from single-engined variants of Spitfire, Hurricane, Defiant, Lysander, Typhoon and Mustang I to twin-engined Blenheims, Beaufighters, Whirlwinds and Havocs etc., with an assortment of types one had never seen before, let alone flown. It was not unusual to fly three or four entirely different types of aircraft during a day's work.

Lysander

Defiant

This required considerable competence and a reasonable standard of navigation, which was a closed book to most of the pilots, many of whom had difficulty in holding a map the right way up, let alone reading it well enough to get from A to B. Add bad weather to this and they were lost within minutes of take-off.

The unit had been 'lumbered' with a few squadron cast-offs, inexperienced, raw, and below-standard on type and quite incapable of flying the variety of aircraft that the job required. These had to be disposed of rapidly but I was fortunate in having a hard-core of good pilots. Add an assortment of Polish, Czech, American, Free French, Belgian and Dutch flying types and we had a magnificent assortment.

The attitude of some of these 'characters' rather took one aback at first. When asked if they had flown a particular aircraft, one would get the casual answer, "Iss aeroplane, yes? I fly it, OK?" Actually, quite a few were excellent pilots with many flying hours and were completely at ease in anything within reason after a look at the pilot's notes applicable to the aircraft and a quick cockpit check.

Their navigation, even in the foulest weather was excellent and bad conditions were generally dismissed on their return with the remark "The weather? Iss alright," often when it was so bad that even the birds were walking.

On one occasion, I received a telephone call from an irate civilian employee responsible for releasing aircraft at one of the MUs in the Cotswolds. "There's a bloody foreigner here, can't speak proper English and wants a Spitfire, says he's from you and I'm not going to, etc. etc."

I had to interrupt, and with my infinite capacity for pouring oil on troubled waters, using as openers that crushing and original phrase, "Don't you know there's a bloody war on? Of course he can't understand your English, he's in Gloucestershire, isn't he? He's got the right authorisation and unless he signs for it as Hitler or Goering you'd better let him have it and quickly.

Later I had the opportunity to apologise for my rudeness to the old boy at the MU and he very nobly forgave me. Having put down the telephone the thought struck home that Hitler and Goering would have bid good money for that Spitfire. Galland the German Fighter Ace, when asked by Hitler what his requirements were to sway the air struggle in Germany's favour, had replied, "A Squadron of Spitfires."

I tried hard to improve the efficiency of No. 1 ADF, getting more pilots with the ability to cope with a demanding job, and increasing the number of transport aircraft for which work the Dominie was ideally suited. As long as the weather countrywide was just flyable we were able to keep the increasing flow on the movements board cleared daily, which I think pleased Command.

It became apparent that, to cope with increasing traffic, the overnight stop-over of aircraft in transit, and the limited facilities available at Hendon, a move to a larger airfield, was necessary. In any case, although no operational flying or night flying now took place there, it was obvious that the unit was, to say the least, not encouraged. This was borne out on two specific occasions. The first occurred when Jackie Mann, of whom more later, was flying a Spitfire from

Lincolnshire to a southern airfield, Tangmere, I think. It was Christmas Eve afternoon, a foul day with very low cloud and poor visibility. Having been delayed Jackie rang prior to take off and asked if he could land at Hendon for the night if he could not get down to Tangmere before dark, to which I agreed.

The light was failing and rain scudded across the airfield as Jackie's Spitfire roared low into the circuit, touched down and taxied in. It was a good competent effort by a very skilful pilot, who took no unnecessary risks, and he deserved the pleasure of Christmas Eve with his fiancee Sunny, and friends, but I was told to report to the Station CO where he informed me that no night flying facilities existed at Hendon and my pilots were attracting enemy attack, etc., etc., and I received a colossal, and I thought unjustified, ticking off.

On the second occasion I was flying the Dominie late one afternoon, from an 8.00 am take-off, returning with a load of pilots from a job that had taken us all day to complete. The pilots were tired and we were all very hungry, not having stopped to eat since take-off that morning and I was determined to get them back to Hendon.

The weather was bad which was nothing unusual and the light was going as I flew low between Hemel Hempstead and St Albans, passing east of Watford and picking up the Edgware Road. I was at '0' feet with my headlamp on as I found Colindale Avenue, turned hard left, soared just over Colindate Underground Station and dropped on to the airfield.

The pilots were grateful that they had not to spend another night away. I was pleased, but I was in for another shock when I was again sent for unexpectedly by the CO, who went into an angry diatribe which passed over my unruffled head, as all he was saying was that one should not do this, that or the other very often, and preferably not at all, ignoring the calculated and justified risks of the urgent operation of our unit. That day, a typical one, we had partly re-equipped two Spitfire Squadrons, collecting new aircraft from distant MUs delivering them, collecting the squadron's old aircraft and taking them to two OTUs for training purposes, a long tiring day involving me in some nine hours of flying dodging from airfield to airfield. My leg ached and wept like mad and I felt completely drained, raising no fruitless argument with a man who obviously considered the War an irritation, and wished no part of it. A right bloody ostrich. So I went up to town where I knew the German bombers above made it very obvious whose side they were on.

At this time our crew-room was very sparsely equipped with furniture and my formal requests for more met with ill-disguised obstruction. Something had to be done and the opportunity arose when we cornered Asher Rebak, a Home Guard Officer, who had been given the odd ride in our transport aircraft and was a grand type.

His business was in the East End of London and being Jewish he knew all the right people. He told us to get a large van which we managed to hire and despatched it, early one morning in the charge of F/O Willy Wyatt and a driver, to meet Asher.

The van arrived back in the late afternoon with Willy as tight a a tick and the driver not much better. We opened the large rear doors to see suites of furniture, tables and chairs in profusion, piled up to the roof. Apparently Asher had taken Willy to all the Jewish furniture people in the East End and they had all freely donated a colossal load without hesitation, getting Willy into a terrible state into the bargain. Remarkable people.

The pilots set to work and our crew-room and the airmen's restroom were soon resplendent with new furniture, as luxurious as any lounge in the Savoy or the Ritz. The residue, of which there was an enormous amount, was piled back into the van and taken somewhere and sold. The cash being added to our Line-book fund which was a bit low at that time. A sour note and not unexpected, was the objection of the Equipment Officer that we take our own furniture when eventually we left.

The Line-book was a general squadron practice to provide money for a monthly 'thrash'. Any pilot who 'shot a line', bragging of his flying, success with women, or put up a 'black', was put in the book in detail and fined according to the size of the 'line' by his peers, against which there was no appeal.

There must be many Line-books, treasured by ex RAF types, kept in dark safe places, as their publication would bring a blush to the face of the devil.

Shortly afterwards I obtained permission to move No. 1 ADF to Croydon, the old pre War grass airfield south of London from where Imperial Airways had, with Handley Page airliners operated the first European air traffic in the gentle luxury of wonderful sedate biplane airliners, which set the examples of courtesy and attention sadly missing on many of the jetliners of today.

Croydon had been badly bombed in 1940, the hangars on the north side being almost completely demolished. The large modern terminal building still stood, damaged in the upper storeys but usable, so we ensconced ourselves in great comfort with some of our lovely furniture in part of the ground floor complex.

By this time I had a strength of some 30 plus pilots, most of whom were most capable on all types of single and twin-engined aircraft in all weathers, enjoying the experience of flying two or three different types across the UK in a day. We had very few incidents and were now moving as many aircraft as the three other ADFs put together, and more quickly too, which was most gratifying.

There were, of course, pilots who, though basically sound couldn't or wouldn't think clearly and did stupid things. One, a Polish NCO, left in a Spitfire from Croydon for the West Country and, lifting his tail too high on take-off, touched his prop-tips on the ground and continued all the way with one foot of the tips of his airscrew blades missing. Landing, he reported to the Engineer Officer that his engine "Iss rough."

"No bloody wonder," said the EO. "It's a bloody miracle it didn't jump out of the engine bearers. You've been flying on the bloody spinner." (the Nose Cone).

The other fool was FO 'J' who had considerable twin-engined experience but very little on Spitfires. We had to move 9 Spitfires from West Malling in Kent up to Lincolnshire and I thought it was an excellent opportunity to practice formation flying, so, allocating positions I led the flight of 9 out on to the airfield, the FO being my No. 3 in vic on my left.

I signalled 'forward' by hand and opened my throttle gently, watching the remainder keeping position. We were just about to lift off when the FO 'J' went rocketing ahead like a mad thing nearly taking my wing tip with him, swinging in front of the formation and pulling up into the sky and around to port.

We settled down for the flight and I saw 'J' rejoin the formation and attach himself on to a rear section and I concentrated on getting some sort of tidy formation out of the group. On landing I called 'J' forward and asked for an explanation of his gyrations on take off. "Well Sir, I think my Spitfire was much faster than anyone else's as, when I opened up to *full* boost, I left you all behind."

"What did you say?" said I. "*Full* boost, *full* boost in formation. You're bloody mad. Don't you know how to adjust throttle movement for holding position in formation on take-off, in flight and on landing? Haven't you done *any* formation?" I demanded.

"Well, we sort of flew in formation on twins, but not very close."

Shaking my head I said, "God, give me strength," and walked away, the other pilots grinning like fools at the look of disbelief on my face.

* * *

Thank goodness, we had a few patches of light relief. The airfield had several Army-manned gun posts on the perimeter for defence against low flying attacks and, on an early morning weather test, I decided that, instead of doing my usual beat-up of the airfield, to which the gunners were accustomed, I would concentrate on each gun post in turn with a simulated attack. I put the Spitfire into a fast dive, levelled out just a couple of feet from the ground and went into a dummy run on each gun post in turn, pulling up at the last moment and shouting, "Bang Bang, you're dead," jinking violently in evasion.

The officer in charge of the gun posts came to my office shortly after I had landed and said, "Sir, I wish to complain about your attack on my gun posts just now."

"Yes", I said enquiringly, "What's the trouble, wasn't it good enough?"

"Too bloody good," he said laughing, "my gunners couldn't depress their guns sufficiently to get you in their sights, you were so bloody low."

"Tell 'em to take two or three rows of sandbags off the top of their gun-pit," I said, "Then they can depress. You know if it really happens the attackers won't be swanning over at 500 feet, they'll probably be lower than I was."

"God forbid," said he, and wandered off.

Shortly afterwards a telephone call came from the Army and I found myself talking to a very senior officer who politely explained that on the following Sunday morning a large defence exercise would be taking place on Epsom Racecourse involving the Army and Home Guard. He wondered if it were possible to get a couple of Spitfires to carry out simulated low level attacks on the troops, as neither Kenley or Biggin Hill would release operational aircraft for this purpose.

This was right up our street and I agreed to co-operate whole-heartedly. He quickly briefed me on his requirements and as innocently as possible I enquired, "You won't want us too low I imagine, to muck up the exercise."

"On the contrary," said he, "Do what you can, as low as you can, without firing at them, and make it look real please." Such an invitation was not to be missed and I took Jackie Mann for company.

Jackie had formerly been an NCO pilot with 92 Fighter Squadron at Hawkinge during the Battle of Britain. Terribly burned about the face and body when shot down, he had been awarded the Distinguished Flying Medal. He was commissioned while with No. 1 ADF, later flying North Atlantic Ferry and after the War with commercial airlines, eventually becoming Chief Pilot of Middle East Airlines, Beirut, until his ultimate retirement. He was an excellent pilot, prepared to have a go but very steady and reliable.

Sunday came along and off we went to the Races. Arriving over the course it was obvious that the first race had started as hundreds of men in khaki were charging around, firing at each other like mad so Jackie and I wound up the Spitfires and joined in the fun.

The troops ignored our first low run, but in no time Jackie and I warmed to our task and 'poured on the coals'. No man can stand and confront an aircraft coming at him at high speed, at eye level, intent on parting his hair, even in a dummy run without guns blazing. Within minutes we had groups of men flat out on the ground, or diving for whatever cover they could possibly find, the exercise completely forgotten as NCOs tried to rally them to action.

I think we rather overdid it and could warrant a low expectation of life if ever those soldiers met us but the Senior Officer came on the phone later after we had landed.

"I was in France in 1939/40 and at the evacuation of the Army at Dunkirk," he said, "but your performance was most impressive and rather frightening. Very few of our men have ever been under fire and your attack, despite our lectures, made them fully realise what they might encounter in the future. Thank you."

I also had been at the evacuation of our Forces at Dunkirk, in those desperate days in 1940, our squadron flying out from Hornchurch, several times a day before first light until dusk. The Army had been critical of our efforts to cover the evacuation, claiming that our fighters weren't *over* the beaches, not appreciating that our very stretched part of the operation was to sweep inland to intercept the Luftwaffe before they could reach the beaches to attack our men.

For a long while our unit had to operate with a bare minimum of transport aircraft, unless we could beg, borrow, or steal someone else's. Often it necessitated flying non-stop from dawn to dusk, or much later, dictated by distance, time, irritating unnecessary delays and weather, when every movement was a priority and had to be completed.

My leg still gave trouble, requiring daily dressings and aching like mad by the end of a long day, but the pain lessened with time and I had but one complaint – my left shoe was always wearing out before the other, probably from limping a bit.

The Medical Officer noticed one evening in the Mess, that I stood on one leg 'like a bloody crane' to 'favour' the other.

He suggested nailing my shoe to the floor to break the habit, and I'm sure he would have left my foot in it.

I was putting in a terrific number of flying hours on all types of aircraft and pushing all the pilots flat out. It was very gratifying to know how much we were appreciated by the squadrons, in bringing their aircraft, generally in one piece, by first class post. Flight Lieutenant Blanche, a grand character, who directed the allocation of aircraft from Command HQ was also aware of our efforts and soon managed to get more transport aircraft allocated to us to ease our problems.

There were times when the weather countrywide was a complete 'clamp', when no one was flying, not even Pontius the pilot, and with no signs of it lifting some days it was wise to give the pilots a break and stand them down.

On these occasions I would walk into the pilot's Crew Room and announce the good news but, before they could scatter to the pubs and popsies, I would say, like Judge Jeffries, "I have here a note of certain misdemeanours committed by certain pilots, which justify an entry in the 'Line book' and an appropriate large fine. I am prepared to commute these to an overnight train trip tonight to Scotland, Cornwall or somewhere equally inaccessible to collect an aircraft and deliver it and return home by train." These overnight trips were the death penalty, as one may as well be dead as suffer the excruciating discomfort of standing in the over-crowded corridor of a night train without food or drink for 500 or 600 miles.

On reading names of the culprits the howls of laughter of the innocent were drowned by the cries of agony of the sentenced. The well-breeched would stump up any fine to avoid the prescribed fate while the impecunious would slump in the corner, drained of life at the horror and punishment that lay before them.

* * *

Flight Sergeant Wood, who held the outright record for misdemeanours and overnight train trips, and who should have been sent on a few trans-Siberian excursions for fun had an appealing sense of humour, if one had a strong stomach.

Returning one night from the pub at the bottom of Purley Way, The Propeller I think it was called, he managed to get one of the very long bamboo trolley-bus poles, used for unhooking the overhead contact and decided to practice arms drill on his way home. With this pole perched precariously on his shoulder at the 'slope' and which he proposed to add to the collection of 'trophies' in the Crew-Room, he was walking very unsteadily back towards the airfield entrance. A police constable said, "And where, Sergeant, do you think you are going with that?" pointing to the waving pole, which disappeared out of sight up into the night sky.

"I am returning to the Guard Room, to report for Guard duty, Officer and, as you know, a good soldier carries his rifle as his constant companion, and I've got mine here."

"Oh", said the Constable, "that's alright then – for a moment I thought you were pinching it!" And hiding a grin, walked away.

Wood discovered the hydrogen bomb long before anyone else. Well, at least his victim would concede this. It all started when Wood, snooping around the Terminal building, came to the Met. Office and managed to scrounge a couple of the large balloons, which, when filled with hydrogen were released on occasion by the Met. people to record wind-speed and direction. Secreting these, filled with hydrogen, in his quarters, he waited for the opportunity to put them to use. Having tested the first balloon experimentally he was at action stations.

Apparently, and unknown to me, an officer, a very unlikeable and overbearing person, had seen fit to admonish Wood in front of several airmen, inexcusable for a petty infringement of which the Flight Sergeant was innocent. He was determined to seek his revenge. I would not have condoned his subsequent actions but the outcome was hilarious.

Wood had prepared a short paper-fuse below the balloon and, timing the moment when the corridor was deserted he lit the fuse, stealthily opened the door of the victim's office, where he was seated alone, and propelled the balloon into the office silently, closed the door gently and ran like mad.

It was discovered later that the officer, with his back to the door, was unaware of proceedings until much too late, when, looking over his shoulder, he saw the fused balloon bobbing against the ceiling. Before he could move, a terrific blast of air propelled him and his desk across the room in a hailstorm of papers until brought up sharply by the far wall.

Luckily no damage was done other than a slight shock to the nervous system of the officer, who wouldn't ever sit with his back to the door again.

* * *

Early one fine day I took off in a Dominie crammed with a dozen pilots for a trip to Northern Ireland to collect a batch of Spitfires to be flown to a squadron down South – England that is. As the pilots de-bussed I kept the engines running, intending to take off empty immediately and get a good start to be at the destination waiting to collect the pilots, if they didn't pass me on the way.

Taxiing out I was given a red by Flying Control and taxied back, to be asked if I could give a lift to a few airmen and airwomen returning to England on leave. I gladly agreed, only too pleased to shorten their travel time to get home.

Closing the door between the 'office' and the main cabin, I waited a while and eventually received a green clearance and taxied out to the end of the runway. My track would take me south of the Isle of Man, crossing in on the Lancashire coast, avoiding restricted areas, and then changing course to head for Hawarden in Cheshire. I opened the throttles to full power on the two magnificent, reliable Gypsy engines to take off.

I realised at once that the Dominie did not appear to accelerate as quickly as usual. Checking my instruments, which all read correctly, I looked out of the window to see if one of the engines had fallen out but the airscrews were pounding merrily in my ears so I pressed on, and on, using nearly the whole length of the runway before the aircraft became sluggishly airborne.

Turning on to course I tried to climb but the Dominie was flying like a pregnant duck, nose up, tail down and I could only throttle back to three-quarter power to keep above the water. Guessing the reason for this state of affairs I knew I had fallen for the three-card trick and pushed the door to the main cabin, which refused to budge. I pounded on it like a bailiff doing a re-possession.

Hearing a lot of banging and bumping on the other side of the door I could only hazard a guess that the holiday-makers in the hold were either fighting or fornicating, or both, but I was not quite prepared for the sight that met my eyes when a breathless airman finally opened the door which had been blocked with suitcases. Through a thick haze of blue smoke, that best befitted a drunken smokers' soiree, I could just glimpse a sea of faces, equivalent in number to the packed West Stand at Twickers for the Varsity Match, cheerful, grinning, reddened with the stimulus of a lot of the best Irish Bushmills Whiskey.

Not wishing to put a damper on the festive occasion, and

still struggling to keep 'Galloping Gertie' the Dominie from swimming the rest of the way, I put my head round the door, addressing one airman whose eyes seemed to appear to be the only pair in focus and softly enquired, "What the bloody hell is going on, or is the bloody War over, and I'm the last to know?"

News had spread round that station that there were a few free seats on the next bus home, and I doubt if there was one solitary service person left there when I took off, scooping the pool. I dreaded to do a head count, as I know that the De Haviland Company would not have believed me. Stout-hearted 'Gertie', meanwhile, was doing her very best and had climbed a couple of feet or so, so we were still in business. When the Isle of Man came up on our port bow and at a greater altitude, I had food for thought, but pressed on, coaxing 'Gertie' to go up in the world, cutting a few corners and flying at a height, if not below the clothes-lines, low enough to give the washing a good prop-wash airing.

Arriving at Hawarden I would not fly a circuit round the airfield. Luckily, with no other aircraft on landing approach, I flew straight down on to the runway in use, wheeling the Dominie on its main wheels only, very gently, to touch down, breathing a sigh of relief that the excessive over-load had been coped with.

Switching the engines off to refuel, I waited until a crowd of my passengers had jumped out and then headed for the Watch Office Control. The Duty Pilot said, "God, Sir, you were carrying a hell of a lot of people weren't you?"

"Oh, no," says I, unable to resist the remark, "it just seems a lot, but those on the open top deck came inside when it started to rain, that's why," and rushed hurriedly away before he could ask any more questions.

The trip further south was uneventful, being reduced by a few thousand passengers, which made 'Gertie' breathe more easily, but I was determined that, in future, I would only take bookings and count noses myself.

* * *

Variety, being the spice of life, brought a welcome change soon, when an instruction was received to pick up and deliver two of the new Hawker Typhoon fighters to Martlesham Heath. The Typhoon was faster than the Hurricane and Spitfire, of the day, fitted with a 2000 plus horse-power Napier Sabre engine. Very strong and sturdy, it could be used with four cannon, two bombs and eight rocket projectiles in the ground attack and tank-busting role, in which it was very successful later, supporting the Allied Armies after 'D'-Day, and was used to good effect to counter the Luftwaffe's new Focke Wulfe 190 fighter.

Normally we had access to Handling Notes of all aircraft we flew but on this occasion none were available. I assumed that a cockpit check and some briefing on flying characteristics would be available on collection before flying the aircraft for the first time. Needless to say, there was no-one to help us except a Corporal Fitter to show us how to use the new Coffman starters, a cartridge device, to get the elastic wound up.

I had chosen Jackie Mann to fly the second aircraft, he being an excellent pilot and ideal for the job, but he showed a streak of low cunning by saying, quite casually before take-off. "I'll formate on you on take-off." This was prompted by the knowledge that he didn't know which way the torque would swing the aircraft on opening the throttle, and, amongst other important things, what flap selection and speed of approach to landing was required.

As I was, if anything, more ignorant than he of such matters, I thought he was sticking his neck out a little but said nothing. The Sabre engines burst into life with a thunderous roar from their stubby exhausts and one had the immediate feeling that this was no lady like the Spitfire but a he-man, a bruiser, a very tough cookie.

Taxiing out on to the runway I checked everything that could be checked, trimmed everything at neutral and sure enough there was Jackie tucked in to my port wing, glued for take-off. I grinned at him, signalled 'forward-charge' and away we went. Needless to say, we swung a little but remained pointed in the right direction which was the most important thing, and climbed away in rare style.

I enjoyed flying this powerful brute, but, of course, made odious and unfair comparisons with the queen of them all, the Spitfire. Arriving in quick time over Martlesham I gave Jackie the normal wave-off, to land independently, but he wasn't having any. I'd got him up there so I had to get him down, and he made this abundantly clear by closing in tightly to my wing and making a very insubordinate gesture with a couple of fingers.

As I couldn't hold a drum-head court martial at 1,000 feet I made a very tight circuit of the airfield with Jackie really sweating it out on the inside of the near vertical turn until I straightened up for final approach and run-in.The heavy Typhoon came in fast with plenty of power and settled down easily, with Jackie's Typhoon rolling alongside.

We were impressed, but not at all influenced to change our affection for the Spitfire.

* * *

Nearly two years had passed since I had taken command of No. 1 ADF. I had worked very hard to forge it into an efficient unit, and was very pleased that our efforts were appreciated, by the reports of squadrons to Group Headquarters and from where we also had unstinting praise for our diligence.

Separating the chaff from the wheat, the unit now had a large number of experienced and reliable pilots, some of whom of equal rank to myself were posted in, supernumary, for short periods, being rested or awaiting postings to squadron commands. Our work ran with near-clockwork precision and speed, now having ample transport aircraft to facilitate movements.

In all that time we had been fortunate in having very few flying incidents attributable to pilot error as I had, on occasion to take a calculated risk that a pilot was equal to the task for which he was detailed, trusting in my assessment and judgement of the circumstances, be it type of aircraft, distance, navigation ability, weather and size of airfields.

Unfortunately, one incident was to cloud my horizon and give me an unpleasant feeling of resentment, which prompted my later actions. By good fortune, it was to give me a new field of vision and a satisfaction I have long remembered.

A young sergeant pilot of average ability was detailed to fly a Spitfire Mark IX from A to B. Checked out, he had flown Mark Vs and the odd IX but leaving 'A' he decided, without permission, to divert to Croydon, en route, for lunch. Landing at Croydon he came in a little too fast, touched down too far up the airfield and, foolishly, trying to check the aircraft too much with brakes, tipped it on it's nose.

A simple and stupid case of pilot error, but I was alarmed to be called before a Group Captain, and virtually accused of lax discipline and responsibility, which I denied, in terms, prompted by my fuming indignation, which almost amounted to insubordination.

I realised that I was before one of those self-inflating God-images. I was incensed that, after working so enthusiastically, so hard and for so long, with little leave, clocking up hundred of flying hours in all weathers, to maintain an efficient unit, I should be subjected to a venomous tirade that left me breathless, and given an almighty rocket which bore the hallmarks of vindictiveness. I felt for a while that it had all been for nothing but there was work to be done and I put the incident behind me.

My leg, as ever on bad days, was still giving me a lot of stick, but had dried up and no longer required the daily dressings and bandaging that I had borne impatiently for so long, so I immediately applied for a review of my medical category and shortly went before a Medical Board in London.

To my surprise and unbounded relief I was given an upgraded category that would permit me to get back into the operational sphere, but it was one limited permanently to home service in the UK only. This finally precluded my chance of getting back into a front-line fighter squadron which required overseas capability and I was crest-fallen, wanting so much to get back into the aggressive combat role over Europe, the Middle or Far East.

However I persevered and, initially, was told that I was fit only for training and instructional flying duties and nothing else. This was disheartening, but I knew that Air Sea Rescue had now developed into a remarkably efficient service providing search and rescue cover around the coasts and I pressed hard to be considered for this duty.

Again, to my delight and pleasure I was posted to No. 277 ASR Squadron at Hawkinge, by Folkestone. I felt that, though, as I thought, possibly second-best, I was heading in the right direction and was satisfied.

Never for a moment, did I visualise how much this posting was to change my attitude and feelings, giving me a new sense of direction that was to colour my future life and a satisfaction and fulfilment which I should always treasure.

After I had left Croydon I was informed that I had been recommended for an award of the Air Force Cross for my work in No. 1 ADF, but that certain influence had been brought to bear to quash it. I could but guess from what source, and had a few bitter thoughts, but life is like that, the slings and arrows of outrageous fortune, and I could only feel sorry that anyone could be so warped by personal enmity.

Crosses, excluding those of religious significance, whether received for living distinction or final extinction, finish up, just the same, on your chest for others to express envy or sympathy. I felt, if not totally damned, merely damned with faint praise, and left it at that.

Chapter 9

No, 277 Air Sea Rescue Squadron Hawkinge

It was the Autumn of 1943 and I drove up the hill from Folkestone, stopping on the top to look back over the Straits of Dover towards Cap GrizNez on the French coast, now shrouded in mist, and wondered what the future held in store for me this time. With natural optimism I thought it could only be better, and drove on to Hawkinge.

The airfield lay in a small grass bowl, sufficiently large for fighter size aircraft but very tricky for large aircraft, such as bombers, particularly when trying to land in bad weather conditions when low cloud lay on the hill top, and impossible for aircraft attempting to land in combat-crippled condition with engines or flying controls shot away. I was to see some tragic accidents when men who had survived a terrible beating after pressing home their attacks were to lose their lives in the last despairing seconds. Luckily Manston, on the low ground behind Ramsgate, was being developed into a large emergency strip, able to cope with such contingencies and save many lives.

Reporting to Station Headquarters, I was directed to 277 Squadron dispersal and was surprised to see a hive of activity with pilots charging out to Spitfires and Walrus amphibians and taking off in all directions. This was more like the old days and I knew I had come to the right place.

277 Squadron was a much larger than average squadron unit, being comprised of two flights of squadron capacity and a third being somewhat smaller. The squadron was commanded by a Squadron Leader Brown, a charming, quiet man of infinite patience and with a warming pride of responsibility. He administered the squadron from Shoreham, west of Brighton from where 'A' Flight operated within a loosely defined sector, and 'B' Flight with a similar parameter from Hawkinge, the third flight 'C' being stationed at Beccles, west of Lowestoft.

Each flight had a full complement of Mark V Spitfires, specially equipped for search operations, fitted with smoke flares and parachute dinghies, and also several Walrus amphibian aircraft, again equipped with search and rescue equipment for sea landings in the event.

'B' Flight was commanded by Wing Commander Alan Grace, DFC, a tall, lean courteous man, no longer youthful, laconic, but with a delightfully suppressed sense of humour, and an energy and keenness that belied his years. He had a much more limited medical category than I and, despite intense pressure to remove him from operational flying, clung fiercely to his command until eventually being posted to less strenuous duties. Although pleased to succeed him, I was very sorry when he had to leave the squadron.

I had, on my arrival, although fairly senior in my rank as Squadron Leader, diplomatically made a point of my being a new boy in a new ball-game, mucking in with the other pilots, and keen to learn, taking a good share of the less pleasant duties, but enjoying the paired low-level searches in the Spitfires, flying far out to sea on line and square searches, looking for a very small needle in a very large haystack, concerned that one might fly over one's 'customer', unseeing which easily happened when a heavy sea with white-caps breaking could hide him, or them. The line or square searches had to be so exact, not to miss a portion of the search area, which was extremely difficult with no reference points on which to turn or line-up.

Initially, I had the same hallucinatory sensation as when I had flown out over the North Sea from Wick in 1939, the instruments and gauges performing a war-dance of impending disaster as soon as one was well out to sea. This time I was generally very low over the water, looking down with the utmost concentration, turning back and forth, with no time to look at, or worry about, the dervishes on the instrument panel and the sensation soon disappeared.

On the first occasion I was involved in a successful rescue I was very impressed with the speed and efficiency of the operation. An aircraft was reported down, with an escort circling over the 'ditched' crew, holding position as long as possible to mark the spot. The R/T controller at Dover put us on a vector which would take us to the area and after 10/12 minutes we saw the circling aircraft and sighted the 'customers' in a dinghy. Dropping smoke flares to mark the spot we waited, knowing from our R/T that a Walrus was on it's way. The escort, obviously low on fuel, wagged it's wings and hared off home. We held 'one up and one down' positions, one Spitfire low over the dinghy and the other at sufficient height to maintain radio contact with Dover and the Walrus.

Soon the old 'Shagbat' came ambling into view and, picking up a check bearing from us flew over the dinghy, dropping a smoke float alongside for a landing marker, and pitching over into a tight turn into wind.

Luckily the sea was quite calm and the pilot, wasting no time, had levelled off, approaching the dinghy a few feet above the water and dropping the Walrus down with a splash almost alongside. Before one could say, "Anymore for the Skylark," the bedraggled pilot had been hauled aboard, the Walrus surging forward and taking off with apparent ease. I was to be disabused later.

Speaking to Alan Grace a little later I said that I would like to try the Walrus and have a go at sea landings and rescues.

"You must be off your bloody rocker" was his comment. "It's like flying a brick S--t house. It takes off, flies, and lands, all at the same speed. It wallows all over the place ignoring you flying it, and with the engine at the back it doesn't fly like an aeroplane, in fact it really isn't an aeroplane is it? It's a bloody monstrosity but God, what would we do without them on this job?"

As an after thought he added "You'll get bloody wet when you go down, and probably have to taxi back on the surface for several hours to Dover Harbour, and then find the bar's closed when you get home, but, be it on your own head."

The pilots and aircrew of 277 were a very happy crowd, 'hooked' on this fascinating job of rescue, a few of whom only flying the Walrus aircraft, the majority preferring the Spitfires. Among the former was a Fleet Air Arm Lieutenant, Barrie Edgar, who was, after the War, to become very well know on television, particularly in the *Come Dancing* programmes, and I asked him to check me off on the Walrus. He was more than pleased to do so.

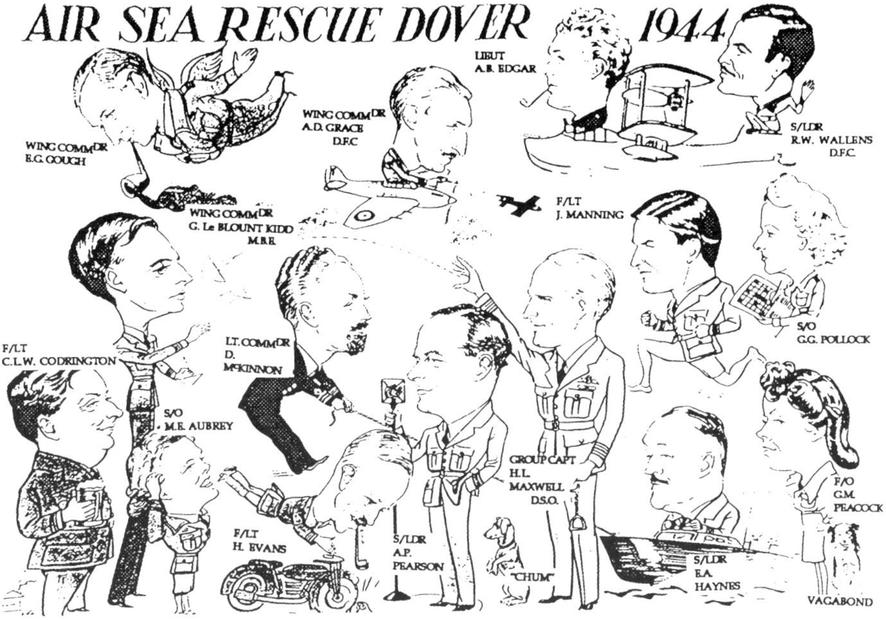

Air Sea Rescue - Dover 1944

After a few landings on the airfield, we set sail for the estuary of the River Crouch, by Burnham-on-Crouch in Essex, where the water would be calm. Sea landings would be left to my own devices later.

To say the Walrus was an unusual aircraft was the understatement of all time. It was amazing, doing exactly what it wanted, in it's own time, with flying characteristics that defied description, but with an endearing charm of it's own, and I loved it. It had done stalwart work in the Navy where it was affectionately known as a 'Pusser's Duck' or 'Shagbat'.

Being a 'pusher', that is with the engine mounted behind the wings, instead of at the front in the 'tractor' position, it rather 'threw' one at first as movement of the throttle produced the reverse effect of fore and aft attitude as with a 'tractor' driven aircraft. In other words, throttle back and the nose came up, throttle forward and the nose went down, but, all in all, it handled well. Later I was to find that the Pegasus engine clattering merrily away without a misfire had the remarkable ability to live underwater, holding it's breath when the waves came soaring way over the top of the cockpit and obliterated it in a wall of green sea water.

Calm sea landings in the estuary were a 'doddle' and most enjoyable. Getting the Walrus in the right attitude to land on the 'step' was essential. It would skim the surface of the water like a speedboat and gently come to rest. The take-off was similar, up on to the 'step' and, holding the aircraft in the 'planeing' attitude, one could hold that attitude and bowl along at a rate of knots with the trim setting holding it on the water until ready to lift off, with, as the book says, 'a gentle sweeping movement of the forearms'.

Returning to Hawkinge, I opted, much to Alan's surprise, to fly the Walrus rota as much as possible. It was a decision that, far from being regretted, was to give me a terrific sense of satisfaction and achievement. That I was, in part, being able to give hope of survival to others, when time had run out, gave me a rare pleasure and peace of mind.

* * *

Although flying a dawn to dusk programme of readiness we still found time to pop down to Folkestone for a few jars of ale, using mainly the old Queens Hotel, where Robin Irwin and his lovely wife presided and made us more than welcome. In addition we would use the harbour pub and drink with the local fishermen, who were brave, grand and very genuine fellows.

One evening we called and, knowing some of them by name, I politely asked if they would join me in a drink. They all equally politely accepted and gave "Good Health". Unfortunately a new young pilot, unaware of the protocol, walked up to the bar, ordered our round and then said, too loudly, "Oh, and you can *give these men* a drink too," indicating our fishermen friends.

He had of course put his foot in it with both hands. Within minutes each of the fishermen walked up to the pilot in turn and said, "You will have a drink with me, Sir" in a tone which brooked no argument.

"You had better say, 'thank you', very politely," I said to the pilot, "and get every drop down, or you will be tossed very unceremoniously into the harbour. You are with gentlemen, the salt of the earth, – or the sea." He managed to survive the array of ale that was set before him, but learned a very hard and uncomfortably distending lesson in the process.

In 1940, Spitfires from Hawkinge had often driven off German fighters attacking fishing boats in the Channel. Since then the fishermen had supplied quantities of free fish to the Messes in appreciation. I enquired if the officers Mess had ever invited them up for a party.

The answer being in the negative I organised a 'thrash' inviting about 25 fishermen up for a meal and drink. The party was an unqualified success, the guests behaving impeccably, singing sea-shanties until two o'clock in the morning, when the Mess ran completely dry. The only incident that occurred was the very rapid and quiet removal of one young fisherman who, in front of a WAAF waitress, uttered a dirty word. He was knocked out with one quick blow by his own father, and put outside to cool off.

* * *

The Walrus intrigued me and I was dying to 'get off the mark' with a 'wet' rescue but my first few trips were boring standing patrols off Dungeness. The aircraft, apart from the pilot, carried a crew of two, generally officer or NCO air gunners, who were responsible for getting the 'customer' aboard, preferably in one piece and un-water-logged. This was achieved by one gunner standing in the front hatch in the nose and dropping a running line to or hooking the pilot in the water, or the dinghy if he were travelling first class.

Walrus take off

The 'customer' then trailed on the running line along the hull, under the lower wing to the rear hatch behind the engine where the other gunner would attempt to haul him on board. Luckily hand rails ran the length of the hull so the poor soul also had a chance to hang on to the aircraft and not be swept away.

If the Channel had not filled the Walrus with water

while the hatches and cockpit sliding roof were open, reducing it to submarine status, it was all plain sailing. The hatches would be closed and the guest or guests, if still alive and kicking, invited to be seated, quickly stripped of their clothing, rubbed down, blanketed and served by the gunners with a welcome 'Tea at the Ritz'.

This comprised hot soup and hot sausages, both from cans ignited by the waiters with a lighted cigarette to a fuse on top of the can. This was a tricky job as the unprepared would hold a can in their bare hand, ignite it and within moments find themselves holding a red-hot tin burning chunks off their skin.

Meanwhile, the pilot, seated at the controls, with gallons of water coming in through the top and most of it down his neck, would stir himself to action. It was necessary to re-start the Pegasus engine mounted way up high under the top mainplane.

The pilot, captain, dogsbody and sucker supreme, was provided with a starting handle, which, for size and weight could have opened the lock gates of the Panama Canal. He had to step lightly on to his seat, up on to the cockpit roof and on to the top of the lower mainplane where, seeming about 50 feet above his head, was a 'dog' into which the handle could be engaged to turn the engine.

Standing on such an exposed platform, without hand-holds, while the Walrus pitched wildly and the waves waved wetly, winding that bloody great handle to turn over the Pegasus and get it to fire should have warranted free trusses for life, but somehow the engine would cough itself alive, leaving the pilot to disengage his handle and dive wildly back down into his cockpit before he could get tossed overboard. The take-off, after such fiendish activity often seemed anti-climatic, but the whole procedure had an excitement all it's own, particularly when one of the rescued would come forward to the cockpit on the way home and say, "Thank you," with embarrassing and touching gratitude. What could one say but, "That's alright, old boy, just part of the South Kent bus service, we pass this way every hour, on the hour, no season tickets or pensioners, just pay at the door on the way out" – and leave it at that.

Satisfied "customer" comes ashore

Dover control would call on the R/T and enquire about the day's catch, always delighted when one could report 'customers' aboard. Landing back at Hawkinge the Station Medical Officer would be waiting at our dispersal and no royal visitors could have wished for better attention as our new-found friends were gently lifted out and taken to Sick Quarters for a medical check and a damned good rest before being flown back to their units.

Normally, our Spitfires and Walrus would be at readiness all day and scrambled as the demand arose but, when the Allied offensive activity was heavy across the Channel, the Spitfires would patrol in pairs on a line 10 miles off Dungeness or the Foreland, with Walrus aircraft patrolling also off-shore, all ready to be vectored to a reported ditching or search area.

Needless to say my first attempt at a sea landing made me

look extremely foolish, although I must claim that poor, in fact total lack of, briefing on one important point was to create an astonishing scene.

Walrus Rescue

Vectored from Dungeness for 30 miles in a south-easterly direction I arrived on the scene where an American Flying Fortress had ditched, and sighted nine men in a large dinghy and, some distance away, one man in the water. My first concern was for the latter and quickly dropping a smoke flare for wind direction, pulled the Walrus round to land in a calmish sea. So far, so good and I taxied up to the poor chap, as if to the manner born, where the gunner in the front hatch dropped him a line to trail him to the back hatch for hauling aboard.

No one had taken the trouble to tell me that it was essential to switch of the engine at this point and restart later, and the Walrus, even throttled back, was proceeding under steam and the gunners were unable to grab the poor chap. I was apparently towing him down the Channel clinging desperately to our life-line. I was unsighted to the rear and mistook the yelling of the gunners to be shouts of encouragement, when in fact they were cursing me for not shutting off as they tried to haul on the rope to pull him in.

Fortunately they managed to get him aboard before he had become totally waterlogged. Meanwhile a Walrus from Shoreham had arrived and picked up the other survivors in the dinghy. They tried to take off but were unsuccessful and had to wait for a high speed rescue launch from Dover to take them in tow.

H.S.L. (High Speed Launch) Dover ASR

Not wishing to make any more stupid mistakes that day I cautiously opened my throttle and got the Walrus airborne for Hawkinge. My 'customer' bore me no animosity and, being little the worse for wear, admitted that it had been, to say the least, quite exciting.

Persevering with the Walrus, to which I had become very attached, we carried out searches which extended far down and very close to the French coast past Dieppe to Fécamp and up the Belgian coast past Ostend, Zeebrugge to Walcheren hunting for reported sightings of bodies, dinghies and aircraft wreckage. We felt intense disappointment that maybe, after searching for so long without success and returning the long journey home low on fuel, I could have spared another few minutes to look, which might have made all the difference and saved some poor fellow, and I knew I was hooked on air-sea rescue.

Walrus in flight

Being the unthinking fool I am, I had completely overlooked the difference between flying the Spitfire, which, except for violent manoeuvre, reacted instantly to the lightest touch and pressure on the stick and rudder pedals, and driving the 'Shagbat' which required, except in dead calm wind conditions, constant attention to keep it on the straight and narrow, wandering about, if permitted, like a puppy on a lead.

The heavy and coarse rudder pedal pressures, particularly when down on the sea, soon caused my leg to ache like mad for hours afterwards, my ankle, still virtually immobile, swelling at times like a balloon and I had recourse to

Flying the Walrus

keeping my leg bandaged firmly from toe to knee which eased the pain considerably.

Having bleated so much to fly the Walrus and attempt 'wet' rescues, I should have looked such a bloody fool and probably thought little of if I started squawking over a little more pain and discomfort, so I kept my stupid mouth firmly shut and pressed on.

As it transpired, I think the pressures and heavy movements required to fly and manoeuvre the Walrus were the best therapy I could have been given to somewhat reduce the enforced limp during the last year or two, but I had to do it the hard way. Even to this day, the leg seizes up and will ache interminably and dully, feeling like a ton weight but, strangely, has its uses as a barometer to indicate rainy weather ahead. Never fails.

I had not deserted the Spitfire, carrying out many searches in all weathers, but the Walrus fascinated me and I was never happier than when Dover control came up on the radio with news of action for us. A quick cigarette on the way and the work would really begin. One day, vectored out from Dungeness for 50 miles, a search, nothing not even wreck-age, a false alarm, vectored again for 25 miles, closing to the French coast by the Somme estuary, the gunners and I searching and searching within a mile of the coast for over 1½ hours, without taking our eyes from the water close below in case we should miss a glimpse of someone or something down there that needed us. One became very tired, particularly if there was sun-glare from the water or the white-caps hid the needle we were seeking. The fuel gauges reading low and a long way to get home, and we would turn away, so disappointed that it had all come to nothing.

One day it was off Dieppe. A Walrus was already down on the water, which was a bit rough, and had picked up five Americans from a ditched bomber. The pilot, heavily laden, had attempted a take-off but decided it was better to taxi back to Dover, and was having a rough time. I was vectored five miles south where five more Americans were in a dinghy. A low run over the dinghy to drop a smoke-flare, the poor bedraggled bomber crew waving as their dinghy pitched up, down and sideways in the sea, and there was no time to be wasted. I pulled the Walrus round in a very tight turn low down as one of the gunners went forward past me to be ready to open the front hatch the moment we landed.

I had done my homework for this and was not going to make any mistakes if I could avoid it. The spume was flying off the wave tops as, into wind a few feet above the water, I held the Walrus just above the stall on power with the nose high and, 50 yards short of the dinghy, judged the wave motion to cut my throttle.

The Walrus hit on a wave, luckily at the right moment and angle, and squashed down into the sea, with an almighty splash, decelerating with a jerk that I thought would break it apart, the water coming up and over the cockpit canopy in a sheet of green, but that wonderful aircraft shook itself like a labrador and came to rest.

I dropped my landing wheels into the water to retard

forward motion and within seconds we were alongside the dinghy where I cut the engine. With some difficulty the forward gunner standing up in the front hatch had tossed a line and was soon streaming the dinghy along the side of the Walrus to the rear hatch where the other gunner, choosing his moment with the pitch of the waves was expertly getting his charges aboard like a fisherman gaffing merlin. Meanwhile my moment had arrived, to start the Pegasus engine. Opening the cockpit canopy I hauled the crank handle with me, climbing on to the exposed lower wing, inserting the same into the 'dog' and turning the crank, slowly at first until I could get it going fast enough to engage and turn the engine over and, hopefully start.

The Pegasus engine with a reputation to uphold was not to be found wanting, bursting into life and settling down to a steady chunter. Jumping down into the shelter of the cockpit I went aft to see how our American friends were being treated. The two gunners had secured hatches and were handing out towels and sustenance to the five men and everything was fine, except for the minor problem of getting home.

Having already seen the other Walrus taxiing back to Dover on the surface with five 'customers' it would seem to be the best idea to follow suit, so strapping myself in and pulling up my main wheels into their nacelles I started to wallow up Channel, the Walrus pitching and rolling all over the place. This sort of journey could take hours of extreme discomfort and I soon decided that a 'shilling boat trip round the lighthouse' was not for me and announced my decision to the five Amercians and my two gunners.

Before I could have a mutiny on my hands I swung the

Walrus back into wind, heading down Channel for the Atlantic and America, like the Pilgrim Fathers, and determined to get the Walrus airborne. Opening the throttle the Walrus churned into the waves, water coming over the cockpit as we slowly accelerated. We were getting on a good head of steam when Sub-Lieutenant Eric Hall, of the Fleet Air Arm, one of the gunners, standing beside me in the cockpit, let out a yell and pointed ahead. There in front of us was a large sea-mine with it's menacing detonator horns clearly visible.

There was no time to throttle back, the engine was already flat out and I had but one recourse, to grab the wheel tightly and heave like mad. The Walrus, without flying speed, leaped off a wave, leap-frogged the mine and splashed back down on the water on the other side. I slammed back the throttle and, as we came to rest, exchanged glances of disbelief with Hall. "We can't be so bloody unlucky to meet another bugger can we?" and slammed the throttle wide open again.

I thought the Walrus might lose a float in the pounding of the waves, or the engine give up the ghost, as we battered along for two miles before I managed to get it off in a lucky bounce and hold it clear of the waves. I had forgotten about the 'Yanks' in the back, and was surprised to hear, in the comparative quiet of being airborne after all that bashing about, a cheer from behind. A cheer, I think, more of relief than applause for that stout 'Shagbat'.

Each rescue we made was quite different from any other, by sea and wind conditions, and also in the reactions of the men after we had picked them up from the water. Their faces were temporarily the open window to their minds and

I found it very moving to see them with their defences down, not really aware that they were aboard and safe again. They had all in the main been returning from raids over Europe, they had been tensed up for hours, flying to their targets, pressing home attacks despite German fighter interceptions and flak. They had to nurse crippled aircraft back until, when luck ran out, they had to ditch or bale out. In a state of exhaustion they were then to suffer the desperate loneliness and exposure in the cold waters of the Channel, not knowing whether help would come before they succumbed to the last test of their endurance.

Some of them would sit in the cramped hull, grey-faced, silent, unmoving, staring fixedly at nothing, hearing nothing, living the previous hours all over again, moment by terrible moment, unable to let go.

I could but guess that others, who now sat chain-smoking, making silly jokes in high-voiced, almost hysterical, conversation, might well have been the ones who, in the dinghy, had kept alive the spark of hope, encouraging and urging others of the crew to keep trying, by paddling the dinghy, baling it out, cranking interminably at the emergency radio set emitting a distress signal that could pinpoint their position, trailing dye in the water for searchers to see, singing, scolding, shouting, doing anything to prevent their friends from falling into a sleep from which they would not recover.

Now, they were over-keyed, over-tensed, minds still running at maximum revolutions, unable to throttle back to normal pace.

How the Medical Officers performed their miracles on all these men one is not to know but, after a while, it was good to call on them in Sick Quarters to find them returned to as near rational normality one could expect under the circumstances.

One rescue, that gave me food for thought, however, occurred when we were vectored to a point close to the French coast at Le Treport. A medium bomber of the Royal Dutch Naval Air Service had ditched, with a crew of four being covered in their dinghy by Spitfires. I believe they had been there for a day or two and we landed in a reasonable sea and hauled them aboard without incident. The pilot and two of the crew were in poor shape but, about 15 minutes after take off the remaining crew man, a corporal, asked if he could come forward and talk to me. He was short, slim, dark and very handsome with the warm brown skin of the East Indies and, sitting next to me, appeared to show no sign of fatigue or distress from the experience of ditching and exposure.

Although now a Christian he had been brought up in the mystic religious faith of the East and displayed a calmness and acceptance of his fate which completely dispelled the fear of death or physical hardship and enabled him to sit talking to me easily as if nothing had happened to disturb his physical and mental tranquility. I was quite disturbed to encounter something I could not possibly understand of man's attitude to life, or death.

My favourite crew members were two very cheerful NCOs, Warrant Officer Jackie Rose from Derbyshire and Warrant Officer Lou Butler, DFC, a New Zealander. They certainly had Walrus rescues taped and worked with frightening efficiency keeping me very much on my toes. Lou had for ages promised his wife, an English girl living in

London, that he would one day during a rescue, get her a parachute which had not been spoilt by marker dye, from which to make undies and blouses. He had no luck until one day we were vectored well out to sea east of Deal, where an airman was floating in his Mae West, with a lot of wreckage surrounding him. We landed in a heavy swell and, avoiding the wreckage were able to get the poor chap aboard.

Jackie Rose & Wally

Lou Butler & Walley

I was ready to taxi clear and get airborne again as sea-mines had been seen in the area, but Lou was still at the front hatch, heaving with his boathook at something in the water. I yelled for him to close down the hatch but I could see his flushed and excited face through the windscreen and guessed what was happening. He'd got a clean parachute at last and, despite my threats of court-martial and firing squad, was determined to get it aboard. After a while he did and then blandly denied having heard my comments to him on the R/T. Later he admitted that his wife had made some lovely blouses from the silk, so all was well – we only aim to please.

Having found a rare old Red Label 2½ litre Bentley in a derelict condition in a nearby barn, the Squadron fitters and riggers were invited to have a go in their spare time at rejuvenating the old heap, which had cost us a lot of money, thirty bob or one pound fifty, to be precise.They were dead keen until told that they could not be paid for the work. Their faces were a picture until it was explained that any and all of the profit, when the car was cleaned up and sold, would be spent on a 'ginormous' party to be held at the Queens Hotel, Folkestone, until every last copper was spent, and they set to with a will.

Robin Irwin and his wife at the Queens managed to get enormous quantities of food and grog from somewhere and the party was a great success. One of the fitters, stoned to the gills was heard to remark that we should scour the country and go into business in a big way but someone politely informed him, "Don't you know there's a bloody war on, you daft bloody airman you," and the poor chap's dream of wealth faded in an alcoholic haze.

* * *

Whether the good name of the squadron had been sounded afar, or we had picked 'a right one', may never be known but one day we went 'hot-foot' for an American fighter pilot in a dinghy just off Dunkirk. With a calm sea everything looked easy, a 'doddle', but we were aware that the Germans would sometimes let a Walrus land on the sea, and when stationary, and if in range, pump their 88s at it with great venom. It had been reported that they were also trailing cork-floated wires, offshore, attached to mines below the surface. If these wires were hooked the mines would surface and splatter anything within range.

Not wishing for an unfriendly reception we went down fast, to make a running pick up, without switching off the engine, and taking off the moment the gunner at the rear hatch signalled that the 'customer' was even half in. Waiting for the signal, I looked out to see what I didn't want to believe I was seeing, corks and wires alongside the Walrus and God knows whether any were also underneath and already snared on the protruding tail wheel.

At times like this there is a strong urge to resign or transfer to road-sweeping or something but one has to sit there, keep quiet, subdue the rising panic and just sweat it out.

The gunner yelled "OK" over the R/T and we took off flat out with all fingers crossed, and I banked the Walrus over and away, very low down on the water. Sure enough the Jerries opened up with their 88s and something came through the floor and embedded itself in the gunner's seat in the hull but caused no damage. The American, however, was making his presence known in no uncertain manner and had demanded to know why we had taken so long to get to him. Considering the fact that he had only been in the water for 40 minutes, and hadn't had time to get his 'Y' fronts wet, he certainly had no cause for complaint, and I gave him a piece of my mind, a very dirty piece, pointing out that he was neither Abe Lincoln, General Robert E. Lee or Franklin D. Roosevelt but only a lowly Captain, and if I had any more lip I would have him thrown back in – and without his bloody dinghy. This seemed, if not to appease him at least give him food for thought, and, on the way back, we got on like a house on fire.

Vectored very early one morning in the Walrus to within a mile or so from Dieppe, we came upon two men in their dinghies, being 'orbitted', or covered, by half a dozen Spitfires, not ours. This looked ominous, suggesting that the 'customers' were important enough not to be let fall into German hands so close by.

The sea was reasonably calm and we planed down on the 'step', picking up the two men, who were the crew of a Mosquito aircraft returning from night operations and forced to ditch and, taking off with some little difficulty towards the French coast, which was much too close for comfort, we headed back for home. The Spitfire escort reported that there were four FW 190 fighters approaching and advised rapid evasive action.

Information on how the hell I was supposed to evade the latest German fighters with a Walrus 50 feet above the water was not forthcoming, but Lou Butler, the stout-hearted, opened the back hatch, mounted his single pop-gun, that wouldn't have knocked a duck over in a shooting gallery, let alone shoot down four FW 190s, and prepared to repel boarders. Luckily they peeled off, flew over the top of us and headed away, probably thinking the Walrus was just a most unusual mirage, with the Spitfires in pursuit.

Our 'customers' must indeed have been important, a Wing Commander and a Flight Lieutenant who, in fine fettle, were whisked away the moment we landed back at Hawkinge, and flown immediately back to their squadron.

The Wing/Co had remarked on the way back that they had sat in their dinghies since dawn, listening to the ringing of bells inland from the coast and wondering if they would be unlucky enough to drift ashore. I said that they were so close to the shore when we arrived that they could probably have been listening to the bells of Notre Dame in Paris, and he said I could well be right, and laughed like a drain. I was lucky to receive a pewter tankard from their squadron, which I have to this day and which is inscribed, "In grateful recognition of the invaluable air sea rescue services, Spring 1944".

* * *

I quite enjoyed switching back to the Spitfire for a while. After flying the Walrus it was like driving a Rolls compared to a Model T Ford. One day I was brought up sharply to the realisation that, no matter how well prepared one may be, the risk factor and Lady Luck go hand in hand.

Taking off for a search I had taxied from the dispersal down the slope to the bottom of the Hawkinge 'saucer', swinging almost into a gusty wind as I opened the throttle wide. Meanwhile, as the Spitfire gathered speed I tested as usual the elevator and rudder for full free movement and pushed the stick to the left full aileron movement and back to right full movement, but, as I attempted to move the stick quickly back to neutral position, it became jammed over in the full right aileron position.

The wheels had lifted from the grass and I slammed the throttle lever back as fast as I could as I felt the aircraft start to rotate to the right. Though sitting in a hot cockpit I felt again that cold sensation of anticipation of disaster return. After what seemed an age the Spitfire settled its wheels back down on the ground, the right wing-tip only inches from digging itself into the earth and causing the aircraft to cartwheel.

I rammed the throttle wide open with full right rudder and brake, managing to swing the Spitfire round in a slithering arc before it could smash into the windward hedge.

It was a very close thing. Another second or two from lift off and I should have been well airborne and would then have rolled helplessly, and spectacularly, into the ground at high speed.

Almost the last of the nine lives gone.

CHAPTER 10

Postscript

There were to be many more patrols, searches and rescues, all similar but all different and as absorbing and exciting as the very first occasion. Each with its memory, of the look of appreciation seen in the eyes, or the weak hand-clasp, of those, unable to speak through fatigue or exposure, to whom air-sea rescue had been able to be of assistance.

In June 1944, 'D' Day was the start of the long-awaited Allied invasion and re-occupation of France and the Low Countries.

With the bloody but victorious advances by the Allies from Normandy, deep into the heart of Germany, the War in Europe came to a final conclusion, with the ignominious surrender by the German High Command to General Montgomery on Luneburg Heath in 1945, and the unforgettable announcement of VE Day, the cessation of hostilities in Europe.

Prior to this, 277 Squadron had established a forward base at Bruges in Belgium to extend the air-sea rescue cover across the Channel and North Sea for the massive air traffic taking place. There was little for us to do and patrols were mainly a matter of routine. On the 1 August 1945 I was posted away for administrative duties in Cornwall.

Hawkinge D-Day 1944

I was very sorry to say goodbye to a very good squadron, whose pilots and air crew had, very often in most unpleasant, difficult and dangerous circumstances, spared no effort, or hesitated to go out over the sea in all weathers to search for and rescue those who were down in the 'drink'.

For nearly two years I had shared in the disappointments and triumphs of air-sea rescue work. The seemingly hopeless, tiring searches in Spitfires and Walrus at very low level, in poor visibility, looking for a needle in a haystack, a smoke-flare, a Mae West, a dinghy, even wreckage to tell us that there was someone down there needing our help, with the heaving, cold sea adding urgency to our efforts, extending the search until fuel was dangerously low and home a long way away, before handing over to relief search aircraft.

But I cannot forget the overwhelming satisfaction of finding aircrew floating helplessly and so forlornly in the water, the cold waves washing over them, sapping their energy and the will to live, waving feebly and desperately for our attention and help. If flying the rescue Walrus, one became obsessed with the urgency of getting down on to the water to their aid before it was too late. Not a moment to spare – a dropped smoke flare for wind direction, throwing caution to the wind and bugger the sea conditions, we were totally committed and slammed the Walrus down.

One cannot describe the look of relief and gratitude on their faces, when finally hauled aboard, very cold, wet, exhausted and dejected and almost beyond hope, which more than repaid our small efforts to help them. I was so glad that I had, for humanity's sake, been given the opportunity to use my abilities to help in this work of rescuing brave men who otherwise could have perished.

The record of live rescues by 277 Squadron is most praiseworthy. From its inception in June 1941, when it used Lysander and Defiant search aircraft, to the end of the War a total of nearly 600 allied aircrew had been lifted from the sea to safety and brought home. Many of these men returned to their squadrons to continue operations against the enemy.

My lucky horseshoe, given to me so many years before, had never let me down. Admittedly, the 'clobbering' I had received in 1940 was deserved by my own stupidity and carelessness. The several close-shaves I had also escaped were only what one could expect to meet. But, altogether, from the outbreak of War to the end, I had done nearly 400 hours of operational flying, shooting down a number of German aircraft in the process, and had been able to rescue quite a number of aircrew from the sea, and could but count myself as one of the very lucky ones to walk away, sadly remembering old friends, whose lives had been taken or blighted by combat injuries, but whose memory will always remain.

277 Squadron - tally of rescued

Though coming almost at the end of the story, and no less well intentioned for that, I must pay a very sincere tribute to the true 'Unsung', the men and women of the Services and the civilian defence forces, down to the lowliest Home-Guard, who did so much to ensure victory for Great Britain, but who in the main were unrecognised or rarely rewarded for their actions.

In particular I would refer to the Controllers who guided us by radio, the fitters, riggers and armourers, all the ground crews, men and women, who kept our aircraft on the 'top line' through thick and thin, and to whom I say a heartfelt "Thank you, you will always be remembered."

* * *

Very much later, after being SAdO (Senior Administrative Officer) at Davidstow Moor and St Eval in Cornwall I was sent to a similar post at Kinloss on the Moray Firth, a large Coastal Command station housing an OTU (Operational Training Unit) flying Lancasters and Beaufighters and a large maintenance unit. There I discovered, to my great delight, that two Spitfire Mark XVIs were sitting in a hangar and had not been flown for the fighter affiliation exercises for which they had been allocated, with, apparently, no one in the OTU willing, keen or even able to fly them.

Gratefully, I took one of them up on air test, intending to pass and enjoy a pleasant hour but, shortly after getting airborne, discovered that the large bubble canopy, on being rolled forward to the closed position, promptly lifted off its runners at the front and was threatening to break away and, possibly, take my tail section with it. So I grabbed the front handle with one hand and held the canopy in position.

I had heard the wheels retract and lock but the indicator was flickering on and off and, looking round the office I found that the airspeed indicator was registering zero. Peering over the side I was relieved to confirm that I was actually going forward not remaining stationary, or, God forbid, going backwards, which was a great comfort.

Calling up Control on the R/T I said that I was not very happy in case anything else dropped off or ceased to function, and that I would land at once, or possibly sooner if I wasn't careful.

I had climbed to 1,000 feet and, turning in circuit, while still strap-hanging, managed to find another arm and hand to select wheels down. I heard them drop and lock although the 'down' indicator still flickered intermittently.

The Controller came up loud and clear in a voice as falsetto and excited as if he had won the pools, or a free seat to watch a Spitfire splatter itself on the runway, and with extreme urgency told me to climb to 10,000 feet and bale out.

"Not bloody likely," said I with a dirty word added for emphasis, "I'm not letting go of this glass roof, I may be charged for it. I'll do a slow run past the Tower for a visual wheel check and come in," and, as I flew past a sea of faces on the balcony, I thought how unhappy they all looked. I should have waved I suppose, but, being rather tied up arm-wise, I couldn't even run to a rude gesture.

As I pulled up into circuit, the Controller came on again with another bright idea, "Land on 27, (the long runway), your wheels appear locked down," which I thought they were anyway.

"Not bloody likely," said I again. "I'm not landing cross-wind swinging on the canopy, it's the short runway, into wind for me, or I won't play."

I brought the Spitfire tightly round the circuit, tying myself in a knot changing hands from canopy to throttle and, coming off base leg on to final approach, flipped the flaps-down switch. Guess what? They didn't flip of course.

So I opened up the conversation with the Controller again, who I think was sulking at my lack of co-operation, and put him in the picture. Before he could think up some new strange antic for me to perform, I sailed past the Tower, grinning behind my oxygen mask at the balcony where a full house waited for me to bend it.

Knowing that the breeze was strong enough to land flapless without running off the runway into Findhorn Bay, the Spitfire and I floated gently in and it put me down to a 'creaser' especially for my audience.

'Robbie', Flight Lieutenant Iain Robertson, who became, and remains, my staunch friend, and who, eventually, was Best Man at my wedding, was then also an Air Traffic Controller and had watched and listened to the proceedings, enjoying the discomforture of the duty Controller who was a bit of a 'P in the A', and rather lacking in the qualities that unusual situations demanded.

Believing Sod's Law, that it would probably happen again, squared, I took up the other Spitfire, which, strangely contradicted Mr Sod and behaved in the most lady-like fashion.

Through administrative duties, I had hardly flown during the previous two years, except for a flip in an old Seafire down in Cornwall and I looked forward again to a pleasant hour in the Spitfire.

After a final cockpit check, I taxied out, obtained take-off clearance and, sitting on the end of the runway, slowly opened the throttle wide. The Spitfire tore down the runway, lifted its tail and climbed steeply into the sky.

Having selected wheels up, closed the canopy, trimmed

the aircraft for hands and feet off and throttled back, I sat, looking down at the beautiful Scottish scenery and recalled the sibilant muted thunder of the Spitfire 1, the feel of it's controls and remembered, how, like any thoroughbred, it had a strange desire to please. The Mark XVI had a harsher engine roar, a different, harder feeling of control and a busy-bee urgency, but it was still a Spitfire, and that was enough for me.

The virginal Mark 1 had been through the fires of battle and, as War coarsens everything, had emerged in its later form as a bit of a brazen bint, and I unfairly put it down to the American influence, the Packard Merlin pounding away under the bonnet.

Rolling the Spitfire on to it's back I pulled the control column back until I was diving vertically and held it there, the speed mounting rapidly as the airspeed indicator needle revolved round the clock face and I was headed down for the airfield. "Wheel check, please," I again requested from Control, having no intention of putting them down at this speed and, churning across the grass, a Lancaster bomber of the OTU, tethered beside the Tower, lifted it's wing to let me try to get the Spitfire below it and, before there could be any more odd conversations with Control I pulled back on the stick, zoomed vertically up to 5,000 feet and levelled off.

We were heading south over the Grampian mountains as the Spitfire and I cavorted about the sky in loops and rolls ending in another vertical dive and climb that took us higher and higher until, almost hanging stationary on the milling airscrew, pinned, like a butterfly to canvas, against the blue sky, I kicked on hard left, rudder and the Spitfire, lazily and gracefully pirouetted on it's wing tip in the stall-turn and dropped vertically earthwards once more.

Why had the Spitfire brought me here? Below me the small airfield of Perth, where it had all started for me, lay bathed in the sunlight. It hadn't changed in the thousands of days, or was it years, since I left it, and, as I circled, a kaleidoscope of memories flashed through my mind and it was hard to realise that so much had happened.

I looked for Mr Jarrett, my Tiger Moth instructor, and all my young friends of those very early days, full of high hopes, as I, but there was nothing there to see, memory only remaining, and I suddenly realised why I was there.

My flying career had started here, and here it was to finish. The premonition that held me was overwhelming that this was, as subsequently confirmed, my last flight in the Royal Air Force, but my sadness was relieved that it was made with one of the first ladies of my life, my beloved Spitfire, and in whose company alone in many variants, I had flown for nearly 2,000 hours.

The boyhood dream, of being a fighter pilot, had been fulfilled in the company of some of the finest and bravest men in a front line squadron, an experience that comes to very few, but which good fortune had granted me, and I was content.

I had also been fortunate to have been awarded the Distinguished Flying Cross and I was extremely pleased and proud that the gold rosette emblem, the Battle of Britain Star, superimposed on the 1939/45 Medal, I also wore on my tunic, made everything that I had experienced so very worthwhile, and I turned the Spitfire gently for home.

PRESS ON CHAPS

Oh, friends of yesterday,
        Good humoured, smiling,
Who joined me in the search
        For Earth's beguiling,
With laughter, happiness,
        And often pain
Come back – and then –
        We'll do it all again!

"Wally Wallens"
Stratford-upon-Avon
1989

COMICAL COMBAT CHAOS

Extracts from the concise and definitive guide to aerial fisticuffs

Hints and tips, and do's and don'ts for the budding fighter pilot.

This pamphlet, for obvious reasons, should be kept, at readiness, easily separated and detachable, on a piece of string dangling from a nail in the cockpit.

Should you wish to live to a ripe young age, DON'T ever go near the enemy, even in fun which can become a nasty habit, unless specifically ordered and threatened so to do. Get this in writing if you can. If you have drawn the short straw, then get out your prayer mat and joss sticks muttering, "Oh Gawd, what am I doing here, get me out," or, "Mother, don't let them hurt me and I promise I'll never boot your cat up the arse again," or similar plaintive alternatives which come to mind, or that you can make up as you go along.

This ritual may take some little time to become effective, and you may have to wait all day if the exchange is flooded with calls from the other poor buggers in the same boat, so you bring in your reserve or back-up system which, on a good day can work like a charm. Clear your throat of the clutter of bulbous frogs sitting there clogging your flue and, in a calm, steady, low-pitched voice call the Controller on the R/T.

It is most difficult to do this when your teeth are firmly

clenched to stop them chattering like castanets to expose your terror, but the Controller is expecting you to gibber wildly anyway and your falsetto screeching is the norm. Anything else would throw him completely.

"Hello Kipper – this is Custard Yellow One, I am returning to base," and then throw the book at him. You may be lucky, with one or all of the following.

My engine has	a) stopped b) fallen out c) gone into reverse
I am	a) blind b) drunk c) blind drunk
It's	a) snowing hard b) icing up c) pissing down d) my day off
My wheels won't	a) go up b) go down c) go round d) work at all – they've been stolen

or

"I forgot to fill up. It will be dark soon and I haven't got a torch. Where is everyone? I'm lonely. There's a bloody big German staring at me," and so on and so on.

If none of these blandishments meet with a warm and welcoming response from the Controller you are getting slightly deeper in it, probably hemmed in and completely surrounded by one other Spitfire, pushing you towards a few hundred ME 109s, all with 'Welcome' on their spinners. You will realise that the big bad wolf is at the door, and quick thinking and rapid decisions are a must.

Should you, by chance, have a much-thumbed and dog-eared copy of the Fighter Boys Compendium of all Knowledge about your person or lying in the bilges of your aircraft, leave it there as it may well absorb the impact of a well-directed burst of cannon and save your life. It's probably the only bloody thing that will.

Remembering who, what and where you are, and bitterly regretting it, wishing you had as your people so wisely suggested, chosen a more exciting career of stone-crushing in the Sahara instead of this, you make a split-second decision, which has probably taken 15 minutes to work out, and slowly lower your seat to the bottom of it's travel until you are virtually squatting on the floor. This will limit your vision considerably, in fact even if you are eight feet tall you won't see a bloody thing, but you may not be going anywhere anyway, and it feels so cosy. It may persuade the enemy that there is no one at home today and they won't shoot. Don't rely on this but it's worth a try.

Suddenly, and without warning you spring the well-worn trap. You feint towards the enemy, trying hard not to swoon away in the cockpit. This will always confuse your foe, who then thinks that you don't believe that he thinks that you don't know that he's there, and you don't, do you?

Highly aggrieved, the formation of 109s, which has

probably grown to a thousand by now, will scatter in confusion, chaff before the wind, heading for home and a lump of liverwurst before you can say, "Which one of you shower's Adolf Schickelgruber?"

This, at least, gives you a moral victory and the chance to go home, change your laundry and learn where and how to switch on your gun-button, line up your reflector sight settings, and check your aircraft recognition silhouettes. It is unfriendly to shoot down a friendly aircraft and the NAAFI are not as yet, as you reported previously in error, flying in combat in this group, although it must be conceded that their buns can, thrown even at slow speed, do a hell of a lot of damage.

If and when you first fire your guns in anger having practised previously on your own to master the art of doing it without closing your eyes and holding your hands over your ears – and failed, you may reopen your eyes to find that the sky, a moment previously full to the brim with aircraft of all nationalities, shapes and sizes, some friendly, some belligerent, is suddenly empty, completely deserted, a desolate waste.

You are the only aircraft left on Earth, or close to it and everyone's gone to the Moon. This is an extension of a children's game called 'Go and hide in the corner' and it's surprising how many corners there are in the sky when the party gets rough. Left to your own devices you decide to pack it in and go home, but where's home? The sun has disappeared into a mass of cloud, your gyros have toppled, the compasses are rotating like Catherine wheels and the coast line, which was down under your left arm a little earlier, is now in the top right hand corner of your canopy.

"Yes, you bloody idiot, you're upside down. Pull your finger out."

The most simple and effective attacks are carried out from a close-astern blind spot position. You don't see much and often get a lot of old iron falling off your target and denting your aircraft but do not be curious and tempted to fly up alongside on a tour of inspection. This sort of behaviour can have a far-reaching and very fore-shortening influence on your future, if any.

If and when you are an 'Ace', with your name and silly rows of painted swastikas on your aircraft and the superior, supercilious, sickly smirk on your face as the Media's favourite fighter boy, you will have arrived.

But departure almost inevitably follows, which can and will be easily arranged by the 109 boys, who will jostle to inspect your emblazoned score and read your name on the door and promptly rattle your knocker and put you away with a burst that will make your eyes water. Remember anonymity begets longevity.

Finally, if you have the misfortune to get 'clobbered' don't belly ache. If you can't take a joke you shouldn't have joined.

Remember the motto of the Jack Rabbit, Jump 'em as fast as you can, and get away fast, otherwise some other bloody Jack Rabbit will jump you before you can say 'OUCH'.

If in trouble, or in doubt,
Always pull your finger out,
If it causes grief or pain,
Stuff the bastard back again.

Echoes from the Past

Can you recall some of the plaintive bleatings coming over the R/T from poor lost 'sprogs', uncertain whether they were coming, or going, and, often the latter.

Talk about swaddling clothes, they were more engrossed and concerned with keeping their Spits or Hurris on an even keel and finding their way home, than pouring coals of fire on some Jerry aircraft, and were lucky to survive their first encounter.

Somehow they did and, later, could look back in disbelief and overwhelming relief at their good fortune.

"Hello Blue Leader, Blue 3 calling, where are you? I'm being followed."

"Oh, Christ, it's not Blue Leader, its got a bloody great swatstika on its tail."

"I'm orbiting Dover, there's no-one about. Oh, Christ, who did that?"

"A Hun in the sun be buggered, there's half a dozen up my bloody tail."

"I think it's a 109, it's shooting at me."

"I can't see what it is, the sun's in my eyes."

"I think this Dornier is a Heinkel."

"If I open my throttle fully, I think I may catch him."

"Hello . . . . what time is it?"

"There's a Spitfire behind me, I think . . . ."

"I can't get this 109 in my sights, he keeps moving about."

"I think my guns have jammed . . . . . . Oh, I had forgotten to turn the button to 'Fire'."

"My rear mirror needs adjusting."

"This is Blue 3, can't anybody hear me?"

"Oh God, there's hundreds of them."

"Blue Leader, this is Blue 3, I've been hit. Oh, God, I've been hit . . . .," a pause, and the message ends abruptly.

AN INCOHERENT GLOSSARY OF R.A.F. TERMS

This can only serve to confuse and bemuse an already bewildered reader, but has been included, as a last resort, by Tony Harold, my friend and patient publisher.

He says that it will stop the back cover from bending – who needs a finer postscript.

Brassed off	Expression of disillusionment when everything goes wrong, all the time and only to you and no one else, when the natives are hostile. The other chaps are just bloody unlucky – they get knocked-off.
Browned-off	As brassed-off also, but more applicable to sunburnt Whites – or West Indian personnel.
Eight Brownings	8 very small Girl Guides
Orbitting	Going round in ever-decreasing circles over a selected spot, which never stays in the same place and which one eventually loses altogether, and goes home in disgust.

Rudiments of Flying	The foul, abusive language used by instructors, which makes one forget all the already painfully learned lessons on the simple art of flying.
R/T	Laughingly called Radio-Telephone, a slightly different and less modern form of communication from that invented by Edison Bell, but with the same unlimited range – the next room, yet a great advance on shouting at one another at 20,000 feet.
A 'Vic'	Three aircraft, generally fighters, which can sometimes be seen flying together, that is, within sight or R/T touch of each other.
Prang	A sustained dissonance or elongated dull thump, often applied to aircraft landing, and generally more effective and spectacular if it happens before the pilot has fully realised it.
Wings	There are two variations – (1) pinned to your tunic when young, before you have a clue as to why or how you earned them and what they really signify. (2) Two flattish boards which, dependent on your age, are made of fabric or metal. To give a loose clue – if you flew prior to the

Relief of Mafeking – they could be rice-paper. These really superfluous items, however, are useful in that they overcome air-sickness by preventing the engine and pilot from rotating with the airscrew.

"Scramble" To take off enthusiastically in a great hurry, not knowing where one is going, why, with whom, and for how long. A derivative of Blind Man's Buff.

"Pancake" The reverse action of 'Scramble' and sometimes carried out in more unseemly haste, attempting to land, more hole-ly than righteous, out of breath, out of petrol, and completely brassed off. Both expressions are more applicable to culinary practices, yet often ending in the same splodgy mess.

Square Search Looking for hours for some poor chap down in the 'drink', hence the exasperated expression "What a bloody square." A well-designed exercise which, unfortunately, completely overlooked the fact that an aircraft cannot turn precisely at right angles, although at times it felt like it, and which generally degenerated into such a confused mixture of ellipse, isosceles triangle and the inside leg measurement of a rhomboid, that one forgot what one came for and 'jacked it in' in disgust and went home.

Line Search Looking for the same chap next day. A much more popular way of passing away the time but having it's perils. As a line stretches to infinity one will eventually run out of distance and must try a reciprocal and then, lo and behold, they will have to come looking for one.

Reciprocal The reverse direction of that originally taken, but, as one is inevitably lost on the outward run and never gets to the intended destination, it would seem pointless and inadvisable to attempt a reciprocal as, at this point, one doesn't know where one is starting from, as one did at the very beginning, so it would appear to be wiser to – "Pile Pelion on Ossa" (to throw in a little light Greek erudition) and stay where one is before things get completely out of hand – like running out of petrol for a start – when a rethink of the whole situation may be considered necessary – or a bloody miracle occurs. Surprisingly, it always works out alright with a bit of practice, well, nearly always.

49th Parallel The 49th weary leg of a line search, easily recognisable, as the sea narrows at this point and is called the Panama Canal.

'Customers' Non-fare-paying tourists cum Channel swimmers, dressed in Mae Wests and sometimes lounging in dinghies generally unprepossessing, bedraggled, sodden and sober. When cordially invited aboard one's Walrus they don't wipe their feet, but open the conversation with the remark, "Christ, you've been a bloody long time getting here, haven't you?" Which one accepts as a warm pleasantry. They proceed to smoke all your cigarettes on the way back and then go home. At times I wondered if the War had destroyed forever the old-fashioned courtesies of conversation, but conceded that they must have had a bad day.

Walrusorous A virtually toothless amphibian now extinct, reared by the Royal Navy for use as a three-seater Fleet spotter and catapult aircraft and designed originally to put the fear of God into the hearts of friend and foe alike, and generally succeeded. Capable of flying in every direction, seemingly all at the same time with the one exception, of that chosen by the pilot. Known affectionately as the Shagbat or Pusser's Duck, it was cursed, abused, sneered at and scorned by some who saw it plodding along about it's business, but there were many others who lived to bless it's name in gratitude, and I, who spent many exciting hours in the company of the Walrus, humbly salute a wonderful aircraft.

One could continue ad infinitum with some remarkably descriptive definitions but, as these become very blue and unprintable, a reluctant veil must be drawn – we can't have that sort of thing – can we?

ACKNOWLEDGMENTS

(or "Passing the Buck")

I refuse to take all the blame, therefore I pay tribute to:

1. **Keith Fordyce**

A wonderful friend, but an over-impulsive man, I fear, who, having been persuaded to read part of the early manuscript some years ago, encouraged me to "Press on, regardless." Now, wishing he hadn't, he has tried to emigrate, change his name, endure massive cosmetic surgery, and even have me put down – and I only asked him to write a *Foreword* for me!

2. **Vicky**

My wonderful and patient wife who, unaided, completed the mammoth and virtually impossible task of construing my unreadable scrawl into Queen's English [sic], typed every weary word and now, bitterly regretting it, wishes to remain anonymous.

3. **Karen**

My dear daughter, who thinks I am soft in the head and round the bend, but believes that my book is the best thing since cats-eyes and sliced bread – and I do not, ever, attempt to argue with Karen.

4. **Anthony Robinson**

Author of *RAF Fighter Squadrons in the Battle of Britain* who, caught in an unguarded moment, was coerced to pass comment. His praise is unstinting in that the story is as exciting as last year's *Yellow Pages,* but only just!

5. **Derek Robinson**

An author whose many books range from West Country *Patois,* through rugby and squash, to absorbing works on the War, the Cold War, Intelligence agencies and double-agents.
His two best-selling flying books are *Goshawk Squadron,* about pilots of the 1914/18 War and *Piece of Cake,* the enthralling, descriptive story of a fighter squadron in the 1939/45 War and made into a remarkable TV Series in 1988.
Derek is the most charming, unassuming fellow who will, I fear, berate me unmercifully for being so careless and slipshod in my work but then – I'm no literary genius, just one of the bloody fools.

6. **Norman Gelb**

A gentle American gentleman, a New Yorker, and prolific author, who also wrote *Scramble,* a narrative history of the Battle of Britain, and included a few comments from me following a pleasant and reminiscent conversation at my home in 1985.
Norman is an expert in British Affairs, having been Foreign Correspondent for Mutual Broadcasting Systems and Voice of America, and currently

London correspondent of New Leader Magazine. He has lived in England for so many years that I think he would be hard put to be hyper-critical of anything British – even my manuscript.

7. **Carriss Clewitt**

A very great friend of more recent years who, having been a Fighter Command Air Traffic Controller during the War, and who should have known better, read each chapter piece-meal as it came hot from the oven. He appears to have suffered no permanent ill effects, eats and sleeps well and has been passed as fit by his doctor.

8. **Peter Brown of Long Marston**

A very good friend, whom I must definitely not forget to mention, as he also loves Spitfires, has never flown them, but intends to buy one – and, who knows, one day he may give me a ride in the back, for old times sake.

9. **Bill Stapleton**

My very dear friend of way back in 41 Squadron, who turned up, bright as a button, after 48 years, got me plastered, and passed some pungent comments, of which I haven't a clue, as he also was sloshed at the time. He will probably write a lengthy discourse in *The Times* and the *Chicken Fancier's Gazette,* which should be interesting, and then for no reason at all, we'll have another party.

10. To all my close friends in Worcestershire & Warwickshire

Who, on hearing of the preparation of the Epistle, evaporated like snow-flakes in the Sahara. I cannot understand how their uncannily identical parting thrusts, and I quote, "That'll be the biggest load of bull and bloody rubbish, without any doubt," could be predicted with such clarity and foresight and, being too well-mannered to call even one of my friends a liar, must reluctantly agree.

11. Lastly, to my lone, loyal, yet disillusioned reader

You *were* warned and, **NO,** you can't have your money back.

Cheers

'Wally'

Now just a fly on the wall. Wally at A/C Museum 1988

Firing pieces Hawkinge D – Day 1944

Museum Pieces Torbay Aircraft Museum 1988

Author's Note

The views and opinions expressed in this book are not necessarily shared by his peers and contemporaries, and he alone takes responsibility for any misinterpretations and mistakes.